ESTᴅ 1879
EDMONDS
SURE TO RISE

MY FIRST COOKBOOK

Published in New Zealand in 2019 by Hachette New Zealand
Auckland, New Zealand

ISBN: 978-1-86971-410-9
A catalogue record for this book is available from
the National Library of New Zealand

Illustrations by Victoria Chen

Printed by 1010 Printing

CONTENTS

PERFECT RICE

- 1 cup long grain rice
- 1½ cups water

1.

Put rice in a sieve. Rinse under cold water until it runs clear.

2.

Place rice in a saucepan with the 1½ cups water.

3.

Bring to the boil over high heat. Reduce heat to very low.

4.

Cover with lid. Cook for 15 minutes until liquid absorbed.

5.

Remove from heat, cover and stand 5 minutes.

6.

Use a fork to fluff up rice.

FLOUR TORTILLAS

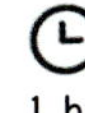

1 hr

makes 8

- 2 cups Edmonds high grade flour
- ½ tsp salt
- 3 tbsp oil
- about ¾ cup warm water
- extra flour for rolling out

1.

Sift flour and salt. Stir in oil and enough water to form a soft dough.

2.

Knead on floured board for 3 minutes until smooth and elastic.

3.

Cover and stand 30 minutes.

4.

Divide dough into 8 balls. Flatten into 7½ cm discs.

5.

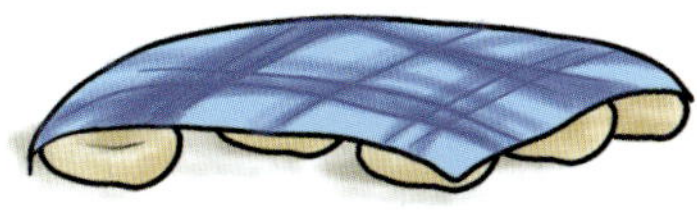

Cover with a cloth to keep dough soft.

6.

Start heating a frypan. Roll dough to 20 cm circles on floured board, turning often.

7.

Cook each tortilla for 30-45 seconds until golden. Flip and cook other side. Flip and cook again.

8.

Put tortillas on warm plate. Cover with a cloth to keep soft.

1 hr

makes
450 g

ROUGH PASTRY

- ⅔ cup Edmonds standard flour
- pinch of salt
- 170 g cold butter, cut into 1 cm lumps
- 1 tsp lemon juice
- ½ cup cold water

1.

Sift flour and salt into a bowl.
Add butter. Toss to coat well.

2.

Add lemon juice and water. Mix to
a rough dough with rounded knife,
then fingertips until combined.

3.

Put dough on a floured board with short
side facing you. Shape into a rectangle.

4.

Roll out pastry with short strokes until
1 cm thick. Keep in rectangle shape.

5.

Mark rectangle into three equal
sections. Fold lower third up, then top
third down, and seal.

6.

Turn the dough so that a short
side is facing you.

7.

Repeat steps 4, 5 and 6
four more times, using short strokes.
Regularly lift rolling pin.

8.

No streaks of butter should show. Wrap in
greaseproof paper. Chill before using.

CHEESE PASTRY

20 mins

makes
350 g

- 1½ cups Edmonds standard flour
- 1 tsp Edmonds baking powder
- ¼ tsp salt
- pinch of cayenne pepper

- 75 g cold butter, cut into 1 cm lumps
- ¾ cup grated tasty cheese
- about 3 tbsp milk

1.

Sift flour, baking powder, salt and cayenne pepper into a bowl.

2.

Rub in butter with fingertips until it all looks crumbly.

3.

Add cheese.

4.

Add milk and use a rounded knife to mix to a soft but not sticky dough.

5.

Form into rectangular block.

6.

Wrap in greaseproof paper. Chill for 10 minutes.

7.

Roll pastry to 5 mm thickness on a floured board.

8.

Use as required for savoury pies, tarts and quiches.

⏱ 1 ½ hrs

🥧 makes 1 loaf

FOCACCIA

- 500 ml warm water
- 1½ tbsp Edmonds active yeast
- 1½ tsp salt
- 1 tsp sugar

- 4½ cups Edmonds high grade flour
- olive oil and flaky salt
- few sprigs rosemary and thinly sliced garlic (optional)

1.

Put water, yeast, salt, sugar and 1 tablespoon of flour in a large mixing bowl.

2.

Stir, cover and leave for 10 minutes.

3.

Add remaining flour. Mix until smooth.

4.

Cover with a damp cloth. Stand for a minimum of 45 minutes.

5.

Preheat oven to 220°C. Grease a large, shallow roasting dish.

6.

Put dough in dish. With oiled hands, spread it out evenly.

7.

Dimple dough with fingers. Sprinkle with salt, rosemary sprigs and garlic.

8.

Bake 15 minutes until golden. Brush with more olive oil if you wish.

MARMITE CHEESE SCROLLS

25 mins

makes 20

- DOUGH -

- 3 cups Edmonds standard flour
- 4½ tsp Edmonds baking powder
- ¼ tsp salt
- 50 g butter
- 1–1½ cups milk

- FILLING -

- 2 tbsp melted butter
- 2–3 tbsp Marmite
- ¾ cup grated cheese

1.

Preheat oven to 200°C.
Grease or line a baking tray.

2.

Sift flour, baking powder
and salt into a bowl.

3.

Rub in butter with fingertips until all
looks like fine breadcrumbs. Add milk.

4.

Quickly mix with a rounded knife to a
soft dough. Transfer to a floured board.

5.

Roll dough into a 30 cm square.
Brush with melted butter.

6.

Smear on Marmite. Top with grated
cheese. Leave a bare strip along one edge.

7.

Roll into a log, finishing at
the bare edge. Press to seal.
Cut into 20 slices.

8.

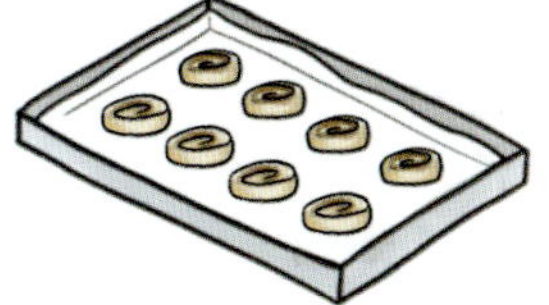

Put on tray, cut side down.
Bake for 12 minutes until golden.
Cool on wire rack.

40 mins

makes
30

CHEESE STRAWS

- 1 quantity Cheese Pastry (see page 5)
- ⅛ tsp dry mustard
- 1 egg, beaten

1.

Preheat oven to 190°C.
Grease or line a baking tray.

2.

When making Cheese Pastry, add
mustard to dry ingredients and
replace milk with egg.

3.

Stir quickly with a rounded knife
until dough is stiff.

4.

Wrap in greaseproof paper.
Chill for 10 minutes.

5.

Roll dough to 5 mm thickness
on a floured board.

6.

Cut into 1 cm × 5 cm fingers.

7.

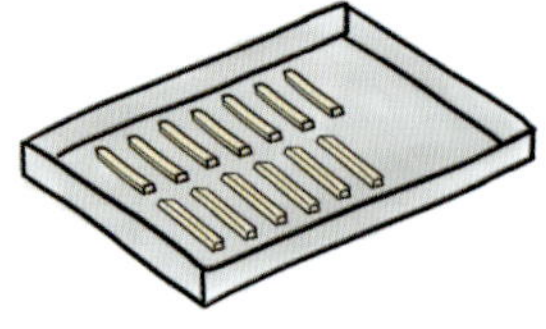

Place cheese straws on prepared tray.

8.

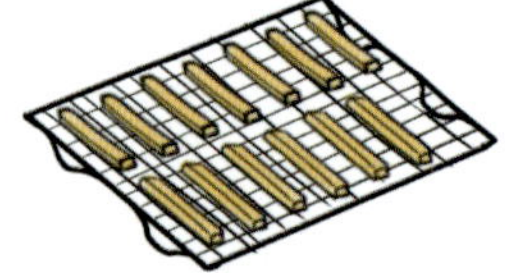

Bake 10 minutes until pale golden.
Cool on wire rack.

SWEETCORN FRITTERS

 20 mins

 serves 6

- ¾ cup Edmonds standard flour
- 1 tsp Edmonds baking powder
- ½ tsp salt
- ½ tsp pepper
- 1 egg
- 440 g can cream-style sweetcorn
- 2 tbsp oil
- tomato or chilli sauce and sour cream

1.

Sift flour, baking powder, salt and pepper into a bowl.

2.

Add egg and mix to combine. Stir in sweetcorn.

3.

Set aside for 10 minutes.

4.

Heat oil in a frypan. Drop in large tablespoonfuls of mixture.

5.

Cook until golden underneath.

6.

Turn with a spatula and cook other side.

7.

Rest on paper towels.

8.

Serve hot with tomato or chilli sauce and a dollop of sour cream.

BACON & EGG PIE

- 2 sheets Edmonds flaky puff pastry, thawed

- FILLING -
- 225 g lean bacon, sliced into large pieces
- 6 eggs, at room temperature
- salt and pepper
- milk or beaten egg

1.

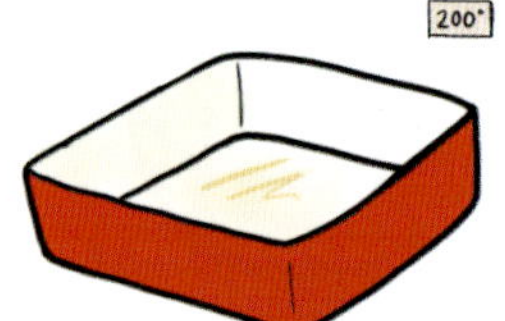

Preheat oven to 200°C. Grease a 20 cm shallow square pie dish.

2.

Line dish with 1 sheet of pastry.

3.

Arrange bacon pieces evenly over pastry base. Break in eggs. Prick yolks lightly.

4.

Season with salt and pepper. Brush pastry edges with water.

5.

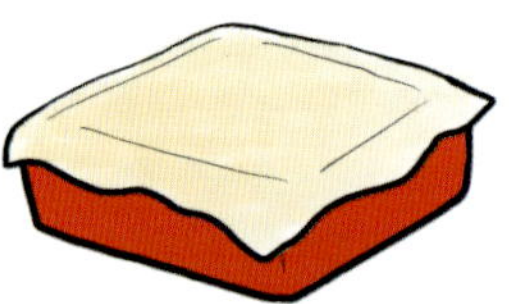

Take the second pastry sheet and carefully lift onto filling. Press pastry edges together to seal.

6.

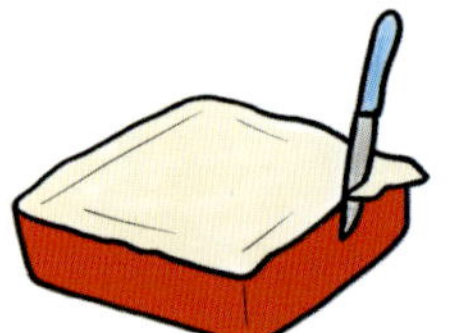

Cut excess pastry from around edges with a sharp knife. Place in a stack and re-roll.

7.

Cut out leaves or other shapes. Stick on top of the pie with a little water. Make 2 slits in the top.

8.

Brush with milk or a little beaten egg. Bake for 30 minutes until golden brown.

MINCE PIE

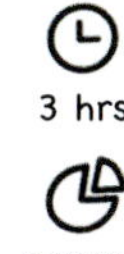

3 hrs

serves
9

- 1 onion, finely chopped
- 2 cloves garlic, crushed
- 1 tbsp oil
- 500 g lean beef mince
- 1½ tbsp Edmonds standard flour
- ½ cup beef stock
- 2 tbsp tomato paste
- salt and pepper
- 1 sheet Edmonds savoury short pastry, thawed
- 1 sheet Edmonds flaky puff pastry, thawed
- 1 egg yolk, at room temperature
- 1 tbsp water

1.

Gently fry onion and garlic in oil for 15 minutes. Stir until onion is golden. Add beef mince.

2.

Increase heat. Cook quickly until meat is browned and crumbly. Add flour. Stir for 30 seconds.

3.

Gradually add stock. Boil. Stir constantly. Add tomato paste, salt and pepper.

4.

Simmer 10 minutes. Set aside to cool.

5.

Preheat oven to 200°C. Line a greased 22 cm pie dish with a short pastry sheet. Wet the edges.

6.

Spoon in meat filling. Carefully place puff pastry sheet over the filling. Press edges to seal.

7.

Combine egg yolk and water. Brush on top of the pie. Make two slits in the top.

8.

Bake 25 minutes until dark golden brown.

40 mins

serves 6

PUMPKIN SOUP

- 1 onion, chopped
- 1 tbsp oil
- 750 g pumpkin, peeled and chopped
- 1 large potato, peeled and chopped
- 4 cups vegetable stock
- salt and pepper
- pinch of nutmeg

1.

In a large pot gently cook onion in oil for 10 minutes until translucent.

2.

Add pumpkin, potato and stock.

3.

Bring slowly to the boil.

4.

Partly cover. Cook gently for 20 minutes until vegetables are soft.

5.

Remove ½ cup of liquid and set aside.

6.

Purée soup in a blender.

7.

Add reserved stock if you want to thin the soup.

8.

Season with salt, pepper and nutmeg and serve.

BEEF NOODLE SOUP

20 mins

serves 2

- 150 g packet of egg noodles
- 1 cup beef stock
- 1 beef schnitzel, sliced into thin strips
- 1 tomato, diced
- 1 courgette, diced
- 3–4 button mushrooms, sliced
- fish sauce, to taste
- sweet chilli sauce, to taste
- lemon wedge
- chopped fresh herbs such as coriander and mint

1.

Cook egg noodles as per packet instructions. Drain and set aside.

2.

Place beef stock in a saucepan over medium–high heat.

3.

Bring to the boil. Drop beef schnitzel into the boiling stock.

4.

Add tomato, courgette and mushrooms. Cook for 8-10 minutes.

5.

Flavour with fish sauce and sweet chilli sauce to taste. Start with 1 teaspoon of each.

6.

When ready to serve, drop in egg noodles.

7.

Stir to mix.

8.

Serve in a bowl. Add a light squeeze of lemon juice, and fresh chopped herbs.

1 hr

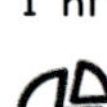
serves
4-6

IMPOSSIBLE QUICHE

- 3 eggs, at room temperature
- ½ cup Edmonds self-raising flour
- 1 cup grated aged cheddar cheese
- 1 tbsp oil
- 1½ cups milk

- 1 onion, finely chopped
- 2 rashers of bacon, rind removed, chopped (optional)
- chopped parsley, corn, sliced mushrooms (optional)

1.

Preheat oven to 180°C. Grease a quiche dish. Place in oven to warm.

2.

Place all ingredients (except optional items like bacon) in a large bowl.

3.

Whisk vigorously for 1 minute.

4.

Pour into warmed, greased quiche dish. Add bacon, if using.

5.

Add a few tablespoons of chopped vegetables, if using.

6.

Place in oven and bake for 45 minutes.

SPAGHETTI & CHEESE TOASTIES

10 mins

serves
2

- 1 muffin split
- 2 tsp butter
- 4–6 tbsp canned spaghetti
- 4 tbsp grated cheese
- 4 tbsp finely chopped bacon or ham (optional)

1.

Heat oven grill.

2.

Toast muffin halves lightly in toaster.
Place on a baking tray.

3.

Spread 1 teaspoon of butter
on each one.

4.

Spread 2–3 tablespoons canned
spaghetti on each muffin half.

5.

Top with grated cheese.

6.

Add bacon or ham, if using.

7.

Place under grill and watch, taking
care for it not to burn.

8.

Serve as soon as the cheese melts.

20 mins

serves
4-6

PASTA SALAMI BAKE

- 375 g pasta spirals or penne
- 2 tbsp olive oil
- 1 medium onion, finely chopped
- 400 g tin seasoned Italian tomatoes
- 150 g Italian salami, cut into chunks
- ½ cup finely chopped parsley (optional)
- 200 g Edam cheese, diced
- salt and pepper
- ½ cup grated Parmesan cheese, for topping

1.

Cook pasta as per packet instructions. Drain and set aside.

2.

Preheat oven to 200°C. Grease a casserole dish.

3.

Heat oil over low heat. Cook onion for 5 minutes.

4.

Tip drained pasta into dish.

5.

Add tomatoes, salami, onion, parsley and Edam cheese.

6.

Season with salt and pepper and combine gently.

7.

Top with grated Parmesan cheese.

8.

Bake for 20 minutes.

MACARONI CHEESE

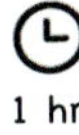

1 hr

serves
4

- 2 tbsp butter
- 1 onion, finely chopped
- 2 tbsp Edmonds standard flour
- ½ tsp dry mustard
- 2 cups milk, heated
- salt and pepper
- 2 cups grated tasty cheese
- 2 cups macaroni elbows, cooked
- 2 tbsp dry breadcrumbs

1.

Preheat oven to 190°C. Melt butter in a saucepan. Add onion.

2.

Cook very gently for 10 minutes until onion is translucent. Add flour.

3.

Stir gently until frothy. Add mustard. Remove from heat.

4.

Add hot milk gradually in small bursts, stirring constantly.

5.

Return to heat. Stir until sauce boils and thickens. Remove from heat.

6.

Season with salt and pepper. Add half the grated cheese, and all the macaroni.

7.

Put in an ovenproof dish. Sprinkle over breadcrumbs and remaining grated cheese.

8.

Cook for 20 minutes until golden and heated through.

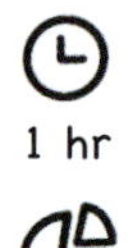

1 hr

serves
4-6

SPAGHETTI & MEATBALLS

- 400 g spaghetti, cooked as per packet instructions

- TOMATO SAUCE -

- 1 onion, chopped
- 4 tbsp olive oil
- 400 g tin tomatoes in juice
- salt and pepper
- ¼ tsp sugar

- MEATBALLS -

- 450 g lean beef mince
- 1 onion, very finely chopped
- ½ cup soft breadcrumbs
- 1 egg
- 1 clove garlic, crushed

1.

Gently cook onion in oil for
10 minutes until onion is translucent.

2.

Add tomatoes, salt, pepper and sugar.
Simmer for 20 minutes with lid off.

3.

Preheat oven to 200°C.
Grease a baking tray.

4.

Combine all meatball ingredients.
Mix well with hands.

5.

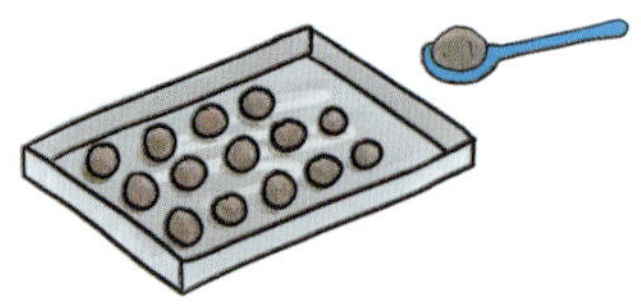

Shape tablespoonfuls of mixture into
balls. Place on the tray and bake for
8-10 minutes.

6.

Serve hot meatballs with reheated
sauce and cooked spaghetti.

MUSHROOM & BACON PASTA

30 mins

serves
4-6

- 1 small–medium onion, chopped
- 3 cloves garlic, minced
- 2 tbsp olive oil
- 400 g penne pasta
- 1 tsp dried thyme or 3 tsp chopped fresh thyme

- 2–3 rashers lean bacon, rind removed and chopped
- 3 cups chopped mushrooms
- 250 g crème fraîche
- pepper

1.

Sauté onion and garlic in oil for 5 minutes over low heat.

2.

Cook pasta as per packet instructions. Drain and set aside.

3.

Add thyme to frypan. Cook 1–2 minutes.

4.

Add bacon, stir and sauté for a few more minutes.

5.

Add chopped mushrooms and cook until they soften.

6.

Mix in crème fraîche. Season with pepper. Add cooked pasta.

RISOTTO

- 1 onion, finely chopped
- 2 cloves garlic, finely chopped
- 3 tbsp olive oil
- 30 g butter
- 750 ml stock or water
- 1 cup risotto rice
- 250 g fresh or canned tomatoes, chopped
- salt and pepper
- 3 tbsp grated Parmesan cheese
- 1 tbsp butter, extra

1.

Cook onion and garlic in oil and butter for 10 minutes.

2.

Pour stock or water into a saucepan. Bring to a gentle simmer.

3.

Add rice to onion. Stir well so each grain is coated with oil.

4.

Add tomatoes and a ladleful of hot stock/water.

5.

Stir constantly for 20 minutes so the rice cooks evenly.

6.

Add a ladleful of stock whenever the rice dries out. Keep at medium heat.

7.

Once stock is absorbed and rice looks creamy, season with salt and pepper.

8.

Add Parmesan and the extra butter. Stir. Tip into a warmed dish.

SATAY CHICKEN KEBABS

1 hr

serves
4-6

- 12 wooden skewers (about 8 cm long)
- ¼ cup soy sauce
- 2 tbsp honey
- 2 tbsp lemon juice
- 1 tbsp canola oil
- 4 chicken breasts, cut into 2 cm cubes
- 2 red capsicums, cut into 1½ cm cubes
- 24 chunks pineapple
- cooked rice, to serve (see page 2)

- PEANUT SAUCE -

- 1 small onion, finely chopped
- 1 tsp canola oil
- 1 cup crunchy peanut butter
- ¾ cup coconut milk
- 1 tbsp sweet chilli sauce (optional)

1.

Soak skewers in cold water for 30 minutes (to stop them burning).

2.

Combine soy sauce, honey, lemon juice and oil. Add chicken.

3.

Stir, cover and chill for 1 hour.

4.

For peanut sauce, cook onion in oil for 4–5 minutes. Add peanut butter, coconut milk and chilli sauce, if using. Stir over low heat for 3–4 minutes.

5.

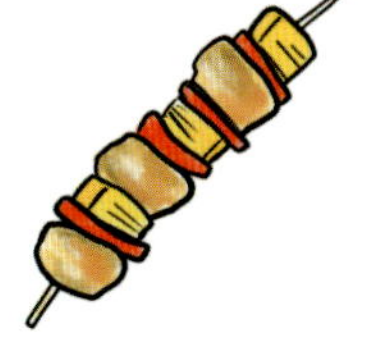

Heat oven grill. Thread chicken, capsicum and pineapple onto skewers. Put in a single layer on a baking tray.

6.

Grill for 8 minutes, turning often. Serve with rice and peanut sauce. You can also cook these on a barbecue.

45 mins

serves
4

CHICKEN ENCHILADAS

- TOMATO SAUCE -

- 2 tbsp vegetable oil
- 450 g tomatoes, cut in half
- 1 clove garlic, finely chopped
- ½ tsp chilli powder
- ½ tsp salt
- ½ cup sour cream, at room temperature

- ENCHILADAS -

- 2 tbsp oil
- 8 fresh Flour Tortillas (see page 3)
- 1½ cups shredded, cooked chicken
- 1 onion, very finely chopped
- ¾ cup grated tasty cheese
- 1 tbsp chopped parsley or coriander

1.

Add oil to a frypan and cook tomatoes. Start cut side down and turn once, until skin slightly charred and flesh soft.

2.

Purée tomatoes, garlic and chilli powder in a blender or food processor. Return to pan. Cook gently in oil 5 minutes until thickened.

3.

Add salt. Stir in sour cream. Heat gently; don't let it boil. Preheat oven to 180°C.

4.

For the enchiladas, heat oil in a frypan and fry each tortilla for 15 seconds, turning once.

5.

Dip each tortilla in tomato sauce. Let excess drip off. Put on a plate. Spread with 2 tablespoons shredded chicken.

6.

Sprinkle with chopped onion, roll up and put side by side in an ovenproof dish. A little messy!

7.

Pour remaining tomato sauce over the tortillas. Sprinkle with grated cheese.

8.

Bake for 10 minutes to heat and melt cheese. Sprinkle with chopped herbs.

MARINATED CHICKEN NIBBLES

1 ¾ hrs

serves
6

- 3 cloves garlic, crushed
- 3 tbsp soy sauce
- 2 tbsp runny honey
- pepper
- 1 tbsp tomato sauce
- 1 tbsp grated fresh ginger
- 500 g chicken nibbles or wings
- 2 tbsp sesame seeds

1.

Combine garlic, soy sauce, honey, pepper, tomato sauce and ginger.

2.

Pour over chicken in a shallow dish, and cover.

3.

Chill for 1 hour.

4.

Preheat oven to 200°C.

5.

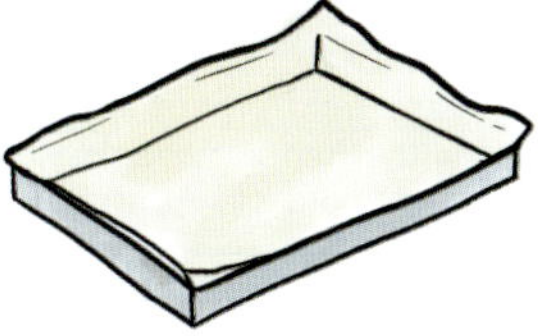

Line a shallow ovenproof tray with baking paper.

6.

Place chicken pieces on the tray. Sprinkle with sesame seeds.

7.

Bake for 30–35 minutes until crisp and golden.

8.

Serve hot.

RATATOUILLE

- 1 onion, sliced
- 1 eggplant, cubed
- 2 red capsicums, cut into thin strips
- 3 courgettes, cut into rounds
- 4 tomatoes, sliced
- ¼ cup olive oil
- salt and pepper
- 6 cloves garlic, peeled

1.

Layer vegetables in a deep saucepan in the order listed in the ingredients.

2.

Add a little olive oil, salt and pepper to each layer as you go.

3.

Tuck garlic cloves between the layers.

4.

Cook over <u>very gentle heat</u> with the lid on for 1 hour, then remove the lid so excess liquid evaporates.

- NOTE 1 -

You can adjust the quantities of vegetables to your taste.

- NOTE 2 -

Courgettes are not essential, but ratatouille must include tomatoes!

OVEN-ROASTED VEGETABLES

45 mins

serves 4–6

- 4–6 potatoes, peeled and cut into cubes
- 4–6 kumara, peeled and cut into cubes
- olive oil
- salt and pepper
- 4 cloves garlic, unpeeled
- 2–4 sprigs fresh rosemary

1.

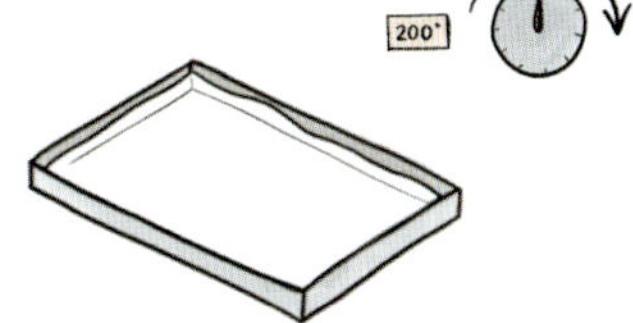

Preheat oven to 200°C.
Line a pan with baking paper.

2.

Put potatoes and kumara in a large microwave-proof bowl. (Do not add liquid.)

3.

Cover with plastic wrap.
Microwave on high for 10 minutes.

4.

Place potato and kumara in the prepared pan. Drizzle with olive oil.

5.

Sprinkle with salt and pepper.

6.

Put in garlic cloves.

7.

Separate rosemary leaves from stem.
Scatter over vegetables.

8.

Bake for 20 minutes until golden.

2 hrs

serves
4

POTATO GRATIN

- 50 g butter
- 2 cloves garlic, crushed
- 300 ml cream or whole milk

- 500 g waxy potatoes, peeled and very thinly sliced
- salt and pepper

1.

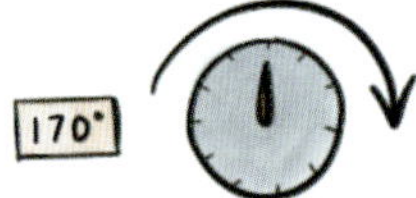

Preheat oven to 170°C.

2.

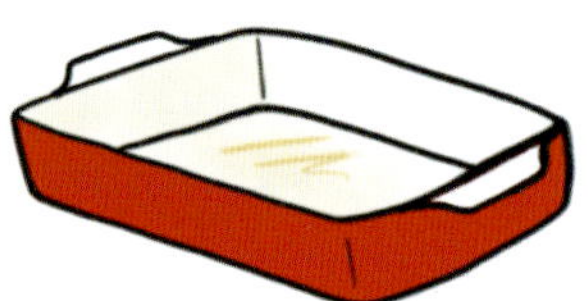

Grease a shallow ovenproof dish with butter.

3.

Heat garlic and cream in a saucepan until almost boiling.

4.

Layer potatoes in dish.

5.

Season each layer with salt and pepper.

6.

Pour over cream.

7.

Bake for 1½ hours.

8.

Increase heat to 200°C for 10 minutes until crust is golden.

CAULIFLOWER CHEESE

40 mins

serves
6

Savoury

- 1 cauliflower, divided into large florets
- 25 g butter
- 2 tbsp Edmonds standard flour
- 2 cups milk, heated
- ¾ cup grated tasty cheese
- salt and white pepper
- ½ tsp Dijon mustard (optional)

1.

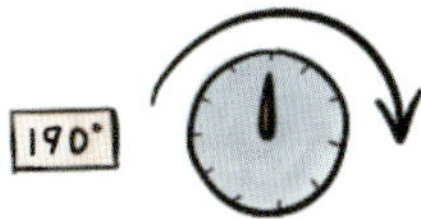

Preheat oven to 190°C.

2.

Steam cauliflower or boil until just tender. It should still have a little crunch. Drain well.

3.

Melt butter in a saucepan. Stir in flour. Cook until frothy.

4.

Remove from heat. Gradually add hot milk, stirring.

5.

Return to heat. Cook gently, stirring, until sauce boils and thickens.

6.

Remove from heat. Add ½ cup cheese, salt and pepper, and mustard, if using.

7.

Place cauliflower in an ovenproof dish. Pour over sauce. Sprinkle with remaining cheese.

8.

Bake for 20 minutes until golden.

1½ hrs

serves
4-6

SHEPHERDS PIE

- FILLING -

- 1 onion, chopped
- 1 tbsp oil
- 500 g lean lamb mince
- 2 tbsp Edmonds standard flour
- 1 tbsp tomato paste
- ¾ cup beef stock
- 1 tbsp chutney or relish

- TOPPING -

- 3 large potatoes, peeled and chopped
- 50 g butter
- 1 tbsp finely chopped onion
- salt and pepper
- ½ cup grated tasty cheese

1.

Gently cook onion in oil for 10 minutes. Stir occasionally until translucent.

2.

Add mince. Stir constantly until just browned. Add flour. Stir for 1 minute.

3.

Add tomato paste, stock and chutney or relish. Simmer for 15–20 minutes.

4.

Boil potatoes until tender. Drain and return to the pan.

5.

Preheat oven to 190°C.

6.

Mash potato with butter, onion, salt, pepper and half the grated cheese until creamy.

7.

Place mince in an ovenproof dish. Top with mashed potato. Sprinkle with remaining cheese.

8.

Bake for 20 minutes until top is crisp and golden.

BANGERS & MASH

45 mins

serves
4–6

- 3 medium potatoes, peeled and quartered
- 8 sausages
- 1 tbsp canola oil

- small knob of butter
- 2 tbsp milk
- salt and white pepper
- ¾ cup grated tasty cheese

1.

Boil potatoes for 20 minutes.

2.

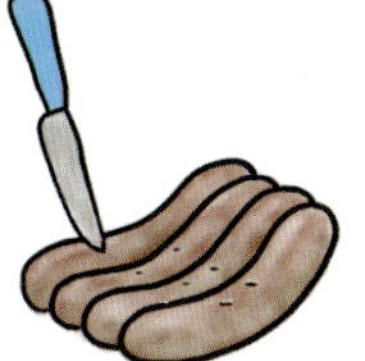

Carefully prick sausages twice with the point of a sharp knife.

3.

Cook sausages in a frypan with a little oil, or barbecue or grill in oven.

4.

Drain potatoes. Mash with butter, milk and salt and pepper.

5.

Make a 1 cm-deep slit very carefully along the length of each sausage.

6.

Preheat oven grill. Pile mashed potato into slits.

7.

Place sausages side by side, potato-side up, in a shallow ovenproof dish.

8.

Sprinkle with cheese. Grill 2–3 minutes until cheese melts and bubbles.

DUMPLINGS

- FILLING -

- 1 cup finely sliced cabbage
- 200 g minced pork
- 1 tsp crushed ginger
- ½ tsp crushed garlic
- 2 tbsp soy sauce
- 2 tsp sesame oil
- 1 tsp fish sauce

- 24 dumpling wrappers
- 2 tbsp vegetable oil

- DIPPING SAUCE -

- 4 tbsp rice wine vinegar
- 1 tsp sesame oil
- 3 tbsp soy sauce

1.

Combine filling ingredients in a bowl and mix with your hands.

2.

Place a teaspoonful of mixture in the centre of a dumpling wrapper.

3.

Wet a finger with fresh water. Run it around the edge of wrapper.

4.

Pinch wrapper closed to seal edges. Repeat until filling is used up.

5.

Heat vegetable oil in a frypan, then add dumplings and 1 cup water. Cover and cook until pan is dry.

6.

Combine dipping sauce ingredients in a bowl. Serve with dumplings.

SUSHI

30 mins

makes 35

- ⅓ cup sugar
- ⅓ cup rice wine vinegar
- 1 tbsp salt
- 2 cups short grain rice, cooked
- 7 toasted nori sheets
- soy sauce, wasabi paste, pickled ginger, to serve (optional)

– FILLING OPTIONS –

- pickled ginger, telegraph cucumber, red capsicum
- smoked salmon, telegraph cucumber, yellow capsicum
- carrot, telegraph cucumber, red capsicum
- smoked chicken, telegraph cucumber, red capsicum

1.

Combine sugar, vinegar and salt. Gradually add to hot cooked rice, tossing with a fork.

2.

Cover. Set aside for 10 minutes to cool slightly.

3.

Divide rice into 7 portions. Place nori sheet rough side up on a damp bamboo sushi mat.

4.

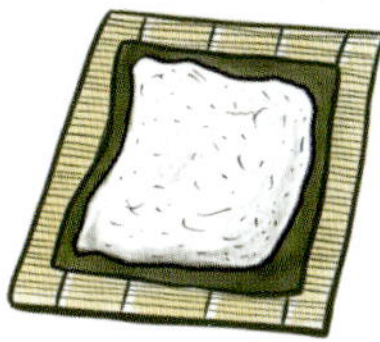

Spread a portion of rice over nori, leaving two finger-widths of nori free of rice at one end.

5.

Arrange finely sliced filling ingredients across one end of rice, 2½ cm from edge.

6.

Starting at edge with filling, use bamboo mat to roll sushi firmly into a tight log.

7.

Using a sharp knife, trim off ends. Cut each log into 5 equal portions.

8.

Serve with soy sauce, wasabi paste and pickled ginger if you like.

25 mins

serves
4

- 200 g rice stick noodles
- 1 clove garlic, minced
- 1 tbsp olive oil
- 2 eggs
- 1 cup fresh bean sprouts
- 1 cup fresh coriander, lightly chopped
- 2 cups shelled cooked prawns or diced cooked chicken pieces
- 2 spring onions, thinly sliced
- ½ cup chopped peanuts

– DRESSING –

- 3 tbsp soy sauce
- 1 tbsp fish sauce
- 1 tbsp sweet chilli sauce
- 2 tbsp fresh lemon or lime juice
- 2 tbsp canola oil

1.

Bring a pot of salted water to the boil. Remove from heat and add noodles.

2.

Let stand for 10 minutes. Drain and rinse under cool water.

3.

Gently cook garlic in oil. Crack in eggs. Scramble for 2 minutes. Remove from pan.

4.

Combine dressing ingredients in small bowl. Whisk until thickened.

5.

Place frypan over low heat and add noodles, bean sprouts, egg, coriander, prawns/cooked chicken and spring onions.

6.

Add dressing. Toss until combined. Sprinkle with peanuts.

POKE BOWL

15 mins

serves
4-6

- 1 cup frozen podded edamame beans
- 4 cups jasmine rice, cooked to packet instructions
- 250 g smoked salmon or canned tuna (drained)
- 2 carrots, grated
- 1 telegraph cucumber, diced
- 1 cup finely sliced red cabbage
- 1 avocado, diced
- 1–2 spring onions, finely chopped

– DRESSING –

- $1/3$ cup peanut or vegetable oil
- 2 tbsp rice wine vinegar
- 2 tbsp water
- 1 tbsp soy sauce
- 1 tbsp tomato sauce
- 1 tsp honey
- 2 tsp sesame oil

1.

Prepare beans as per packet directions. Place warm cooked rice in large bowl.

2.

Add smoked salmon or drained tuna, then beans, carrot, cucumber and cabbage.

3.

Blend dressing ingredients. Season with salt and pepper.

4.

Drizzle some dressing over rice and vegetables to coat lightly. Leave some dressing aside.

5.

Gently toss everything in bowl.

6.

Place in serving bowls. Top with avocado and spring onions.

20 mins

serves
4

FRIED RICE

- 3 tbsp oil
- 2 eggs, beaten, at room temperature
- 1 onion, finely chopped
- 1 clove garlic, finely chopped
- 2 tsp grated fresh ginger
- 2 rashers bacon, finely chopped
- 1 stick celery, finely diced
- 1 tsp sugar
- 2 cups cooked long grain rice (see page 2)
- 1 tbsp soy sauce
- 2 tbsp chopped parsley

1.

Heat 1 tablespoon of the oil in a wok. Pour in beaten eggs.

2.

Once bubbling around the edges, turn over.

3.

Remove omelette from wok with a spatula. Drain on paper towels.

4.

Carefully wipe out excess oil from wok with paper towels.

5.

Heat remaining oil. Add onion, garlic, ginger, bacon and celery.

6.

Cook for 1 minute. Add sugar and stir well. Add rice and soy sauce.

7.

Stir until rice is heated through.

8.

Slice cooked egg and fold into rice. Top with parsley.

CHICKEN CASHEW STIR-FRY

40 mins

serves 4

- 2 tsp Edmonds Fielder's cornflour
- 1 egg white, at room temperature
- ¼ tsp salt
- 300 g chicken thighs, cut into thin strips
- 2 tbsp hoisin sauce
- 1 tbsp soy sauce
- 2 tsp sesame oil
- 1 tsp sweet chilli sauce
- 3 tbsp vegetable oil
- ½ cup cashew nuts
- 1 clove garlic, finely chopped
- 1 tsp finely chopped fresh ginger
- 1 red capsicum, thinly sliced
- 100 g button mushrooms, sliced
- 2 spring onions, sliced

1.

Combine cornflour, egg white and salt. Mix in with chicken strips. Chill for 20 minutes.

2.

Combine hoisin sauce, soy sauce, sesame oil and chilli sauce. Set aside.

3.

Heat wok with 1 tablespoon of the oil. Stir-fry cashew nuts until lightly browned. Drain on paper towels.

4.

Add remaining oil to wok. Stir-fry garlic and ginger for 30 seconds. Add chicken. Toss for 1 minute.

5.

Add capsicum and mushrooms. Stir-fry for 1–2 minutes until chicken is white and cooked.

6.

Pour over sauce and stir for 2 minutes. Top with cashews and spring onions.

60 mins

serves
4–6

EASY CHICKEN BAKE

- 4 × single chicken breasts, approx. 250 g each
- 2–3 large potatoes, peeled and quartered
- salt and pepper
- ¼ cup vegetable oil
- 3 tbsp lemon juice
- 2 tsp minced garlic
- 2 tsp Italian seasoning
- Green Salad (see page 48), to serve

1.

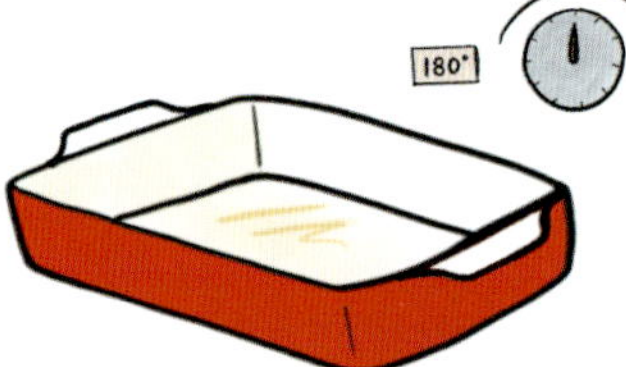

Preheat oven to 180°C. Lightly oil a shallow ovenproof dish.

2.

Arrange chicken breasts in a single layer in the dish.

3.

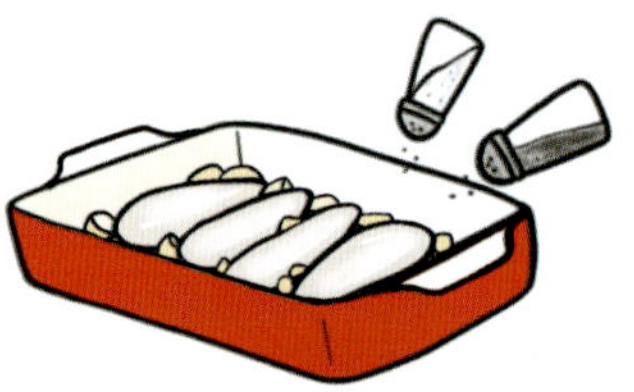

Place the potatoes around the chicken. Season with salt and pepper.

4.

Combine oil, lemon juice, garlic and Italian seasoning in a small bowl.

5.

Brush the mixture onto the chicken and potatoes.

6.

Bake for 40–50 minutes until chicken is cooked and potatoes are tender when tested with a fork.

7.

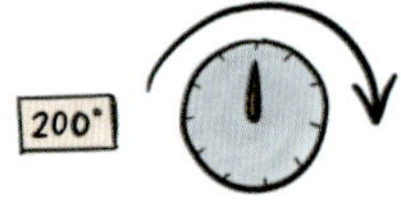

If you want a golden top, turn heat up to 200°C and cook a further 10 minutes.

8.

Serve with Green Salad.

SCHNITZEL

1 hr

serves
6

- 2 eggs, at room temperature
- 2 tbsp milk
- ¾ cup Edmonds standard flour
- 1½ cups fine, dry breadcrumbs
- 6 x 100 g pieces of beef or pork schnitzel
- 3 tbsp oil
- 50 g butter
- lemon wedges, to serve

1.

Beat egg and milk together.

2.

Pour into a shallow bowl.

3.

Put flour on another plate and breadcrumbs on a third.

4.

Dip schnitzel pieces into flour, then egg, then breadcrumbs, and set aside on a plate.

5.

Cover and chill for 20 minutes.

6.

Heat oil and butter in a frypan. Add schnitzel in two or three batches.

7.

Cook until golden, turning once.

8.

Add a little more oil for each batch. Serve with lemon wedges.

3 hrs

makes
2

PIZZA

- 500 g Edmonds high grade flour
- 150 g Edmonds wholemeal flour
- 1 tsp Edmonds active yeast
- 1 tsp salt
- 100 ml boiling water
- 200 ml cool water

- TOPPINGS -

- tomato paste, sliced tomato and grated cheese
- tomato paste, pesto, shredded cooked chicken and grated cheese
- tomato paste, diced ham, pineapple pieces and grated cheese

1.

Combine flours and yeast in a bowl.

2.

Dissolve salt in boiling water. Stir in cool water. Pour into flours and yeast.

3.

Add more warm water until a smooth dough forms. Knead for a few minutes.

4.

Place dough in a warmed, oiled bowl. Cover with a damp cloth. Let rise for at least 2 hours.

5.

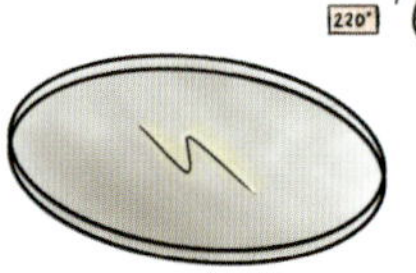

Preheat oven to at least 220°C. Lightly oil a 25 cm pizza pan (or use a pizza stone).

6.

Knead dough lightly. Divide in half. Roll out into 20 cm rounds.

7.

Spread with toppings of choice, starting by spreading tomato paste.

8.

Transfer onto pizza stone or pan. Cook each pizza 10–15 minutes until golden.

Nachos

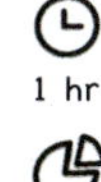

1 hr

serves 4–6

- 1 tbsp canola oil
- 1 onion, chopped
- 500 g lean beef mince
- 2 cloves garlic, crushed
- 400 g can chopped tomatoes
- 2 tbsp tomato paste
- ½ cup water
- salt and pepper
- 440 g can chilli beans
- 200 g corn chips
- 1½ cups grated tasty cheddar cheese
- sour cream and Guacamole (see page 46), to serve

1.

Heat oil in a frypan. Cook onion for 5 minutes until soft.

2.

Add mince and garlic. Stir often until mince is browned.

3.

Add tomatoes, tomato paste and water. Simmer for 30–35 minutes until thick.

4.

Season with salt and pepper. Add beans. Stir for 1–2 minutes.

5.

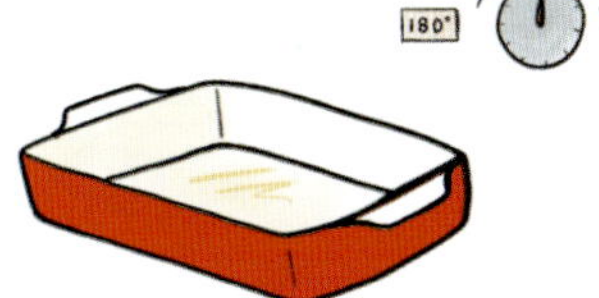

Preheat oven to 180°C. Put a large ovenproof dish in the oven for 5 minutes.

6.

Scatter corn chips over base of the warmed dish.

7.

Turn oven to grill. Spoon mince mixture over chips. Sprinkle with cheese.

8.

Grill for 3–4 minutes until cheese melts and bubbles. Serve with sour cream and Guacamole.

20 mins

serves
6

CHEESE BURGER

- 500 g lean minced beef
- 1 tsp mixed herbs
- 1 tbsp sour cream
- 1 tbsp oil
- 6 hamburger buns

- butter
- tomato sauce
- 6 slices of tomato
- sliced cheese
- lettuce leaves

1.

Combine mince, herbs and sour cream in a bowl.

2.

Divide into 6 portions.

3.

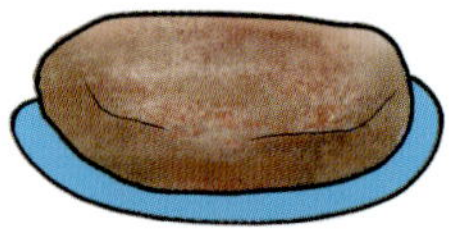

Press each portion into a saucer to make a patty.

4.

Heat oil in a frypan. Fry patties, turning until cooked.

5.

Turn oven on to grill. Split buns in half. Butter both halves.

6.

Grill buns until golden. Spread tomato sauce over.

7.

Put meat patty on top of sauce. Put tomato slice on top.

8.

Add cheese and lettuce. Put the lid on. Serve.

FISH & CHIPS

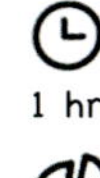

1 hr

serves 4

- 3 tbsp olive oil
- 6 medium potatoes, peeled, halved lengthways and cut into 1 cm chips
- salt

- 4 × fillets of firm, boneless white fish, e.g. snapper, terakihi
- oil, for deep-frying
- 1 slice of bread
- 2 lemons, cut into wedges

– BATTER –

- ¼ cup Edmonds Fielder's cornflour
- ½ cup Edmonds standard flour
- 1 tsp Edmonds baking powder
- ¼ tsp salt
- ½ cup milk

1.

For the batter, sift cornflour, flour, baking powder and salt. Gradually add milk. Mix until smooth. Chill for 10–15 minutes.

2.

Preheat oven to 220°C. Put oil in a roasting dish. Heat in oven 3–4 minutes.

3.

Add chips. Toss to coat lightly with oil. Cook for 15 minutes, turning occasionally.

4.

Pour deep-frying oil into a saucepan to 10 cm level and heat.

5.

Dip a chunk of bread into the oil. Oil is hot when the bread sizzles.

6.

Use a fork to dip fish into batter, draining off excess.

7.

Carefully lower fish into the hot oil, 2 fillets at a time.

8.

Cook until the batter is golden and fish is cooked through. Drain on paper towels. Serve with hot chips and lemon wedges.

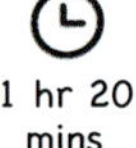
1 hr 20 mins

serves 4

LOADED WEDGES

- 1 kg pre-washed floury potatoes, such as Agria, halved lengthways then cut into thirds
- 2 tbsp olive oil
- 1 tsp salt
- 3 slices shoulder bacon, diced into 1 cm pieces
- ¾ cup grated tasty cheese
- 125 g sour cream
- 3 tbsp finely chopped chives, parsley or spring onions

1.

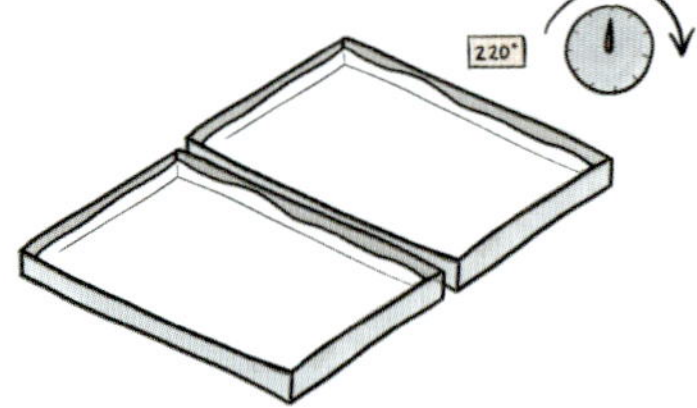

Preheat oven to 220°C.
Line 2 oven trays with baking paper.

2.

Soak potato wedges in large bowl of hot water for 10 minutes.

3.

Drain wedges. Pat dry with paper towels.

4.

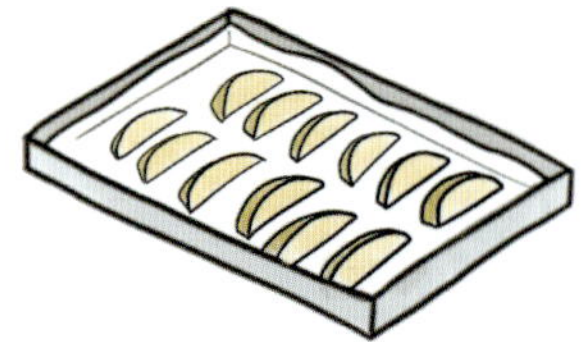

Spread the wedges on one tray.
Drizzle with oil and sprinkle with salt.
Bake for 25 minutes.

5.

Remove tray. Turn wedges over. Return to oven. Cook a further 10–20 minutes.

6.

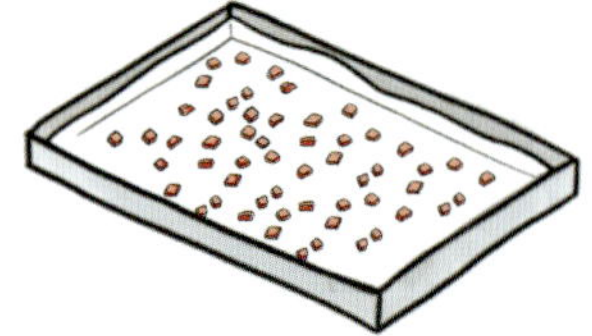

Spread bacon pieces on the other oven tray.
Put in oven for last 10 minutes of cooking.

7.

Take out potatoes and turn oven to grill.
Sprinkle potatoes with cheese and bacon.
Return to oven and grill until cheese melts.

8.

Add a dollop of sour cream and scatter with chopped chives, parsley or spring onions.

HASH BROWNS

🕐 1 hr

serves 6

- 1 kg floury potatoes such as Agria, peeled and halved
- 2 bacon rashers
- 50 g butter
- 2 tbsp olive oil
- 1 onion, finely chopped
- salt and pepper

1.

Boil potatoes until tender.
Drain and cut into 1 cm cubes.

2.

Fry bacon until crisp and brown.
Remove and drain on paper towels.

3.

Gently cook butter, oil and onion in
pan with bacon fat for 5 minutes.

4.

Spread potatoes evenly over onion.
Season with salt and pepper.
Press down with a spatula.

5.

Cook over low heat for 20 minutes
until underside is golden brown.
Shake pan occasionally.

6.

Cover pan with a large plate.
Turn over so hash browns drop
onto plate. Slide back into pan.

7.

Cook the other side for 5–10 minutes,
pressing down with the spatula
until golden and crisp.

8.

Serve with the cooked bacon.

FALAFEL

Savoury

- 2 x 300 g cans chickpeas, drained
- 1 stalk celery, chopped
- 1 tsp crushed garlic
- 2 tbsp Edmonds standard flour, plus extra, to coat
- 2 tbsp tahini
- 1 tsp ground cumin
- ½ tsp turmeric
- ½ tsp salt
- freshly ground black pepper
- vegetable oil, for frying
- Hummus (see page 45), to serve
- Tabbouleh (see page 49), to serve
- pita bread, to serve

– GARLIC SAUCE –

- ¾ cup natural yoghurt
- ½ tsp crushed garlic
- freshly ground black pepper

1.

Blend falafel ingredients, except oil, until coarse. Cover. Chill for 1 hour.

2.

Form large teaspoonfuls of mixture into balls. Roll in flour to lightly coat.

3.

Flatten patties slightly with your palm.

4.

Pour oil into a frypan to 1 cm. Heat over medium heat.

5.

Cook falafels for 5 minutes until golden, turning once. Drain on paper towels.

6.

Combine sauce ingredients. Mix well. Serve with hummus, falafel and tabbouleh in pita bread.

HUMMUS

10 mins

makes
2 cups

- 2 × 300 g cans chickpeas, drained, or 2 cups cooked chickpeas
- 1 onion, finely chopped
- 1 clove garlic, chopped
- 2 tbsp tahini
- 1 tsp ground cumin
- ¼ cup olive oil
- 2 tbsp lemon juice
- salt and pepper
- chopped fresh herbs, to garnish (optional)
- corn chips and vegetable sticks, to serve (optional)

1.

Rinse chickpeas in a sieve under cold running water. Drain thoroughly.

2.

Blend all ingredients, except garnishes, in a food processor until smooth.

3.

Transfer hummus to a serving bowl.

4.

Cover and refrigerate until needed.

5.

Serve topped with chopped fresh herbs and corn chips and vegetable sticks, if desired.

- NOTE -

Hummus will keep in the fridge for up to two weeks.

10 mins

makes
¾ cup

GUACAMOLE

- 1 ripe avocado, stone removed and flesh scooped
- ¼ cup sour cream
- 2 tsp lemon juice
- few drops hot sauce
- salt and pepper

1.

Using a fork, lightly mash the avocado flesh in a bowl.

2.

Mix in sour cream, lemon juice and hot sauce. Season with salt and pepper.

3.

Place guacamole in a serving bowl. Sprinkle with extra pepper.

4.

Guacamole can be prepared several hours beforehand. Store in the fridge.

5.

To stop it discolouring, insert avocado stone into the guacamole.

6.

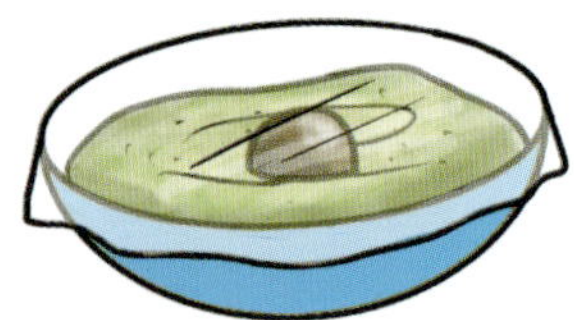

Place plastic wrap directly over the surface.

POTATO SALAD

45 mins

serves
4–6

- 2–3 waxy potatoes such as Red Desiree, washed
- ½–1 cup mayonnaise

- 2 hard-boiled eggs, chopped
- 2–3 spring onions, sliced
- 1–2 tsp finely chopped mint

1.

Boil potatoes for 25 minutes until tender.

2.

Drain and cool a little.

3.

Peel away skin from warm potatoes.

4.

Cut into medium chunks.

5.

Combine with mayonnaise while still slightly warm.

6.

Gently mix through egg, spring onions and mint, or variations of your choice.

7.

Serve immediately or at room temperature.

- VARIATIONS -

Try adding one or any of the following: chopped capsicum, chives or parsley, crumbled cooked bacon, toasted sunflower or sesame seeds (for crunch) and sliced gherkins or radishes.

10 mins

serves
4–6

GREEN SALAD

- 4 cups lettuce leaves
- 3 medium tomatoes, chopped
- 1 cucumber, sliced
- ¼ cup grated carrot

- DRESSING -

- 2 tsp lemon juice or white vinegar
- 2 tbsp olive oil
- salt and pepper
- ½ tsp Dijon mustard (optional)
- 1 tbsp chopped parsley

1.

Wash lettuce under cool running water.

2.

Shake really well in a colander to remove excess water.

3.

Place remaining ingredients in salad bowl and mix well.

4.

Combine the dressing ingredients.

5.

Just before serving, add lettuce leaves to salad.

6.

Drizzle with a little dressing and toss.

TABBOULEH

40 mins

serves 4

- 1 cup bulgur
- 2 tbsp chopped fresh mint
- 1 cup chopped parsley
- 2 spring onions, finely chopped
- 2 tomatoes, finely chopped
- 2 tbsp olive oil
- ¼ cup lemon juice
- salt and pepper

1.

Put bulgur in a bowl.
Cover with boiling water.

2.

Stand for 30 minutes.

3.

Stir bulgur and drain off any
remaining water.

4.

Combine all ingredients in a bowl.

5.

Mix well. Season with salt and pepper.

6.

Serve with Falafel (see page 44) and
Hummus (see page 45).

10 mins

makes
10

SAVOURY WAFFLES

- 2 large eggs, at room temperature
- 1½ cups whole milk
- 100 ml vegetable or canola oil
- 2 cups Edmonds self-raising flour
- ½ tsp garlic salt
- 3 tbsp chopped parsley

- baking spray
- ½ cup grated tasty cheese
- dollop of sour cream, to serve
- handful of halved cherry tomatoes, to serve
- finely chopped chives, to serve

1.

Blend eggs, milk and oil in a food processor.

2.

Transfer to a bowl and add flour, garlic salt and parsley. Mix well.

3.

Let mixture stand, covered, for 30 minutes before using (if possible).

4.

Preheat a waffle maker to desired temperature. Spray with baking spray.

5.

Place ¼ cup of the mix in the heated waffle maker. Cook until golden.

6.

Repeat with remaining batter. Serve with grated cheese, sour cream, tomatoes and chives.

OMELETTE

10 mins

serves
1

- 2 eggs, at room temperature
- 1 tbsp milk
- salt and pepper
- butter, to grease
- sprig of parsley, to garnish

1.

Lightly beat eggs and milk together. Add a little salt and pepper.

2.

Heat a 20 cm omelette pan or frypan. Add a small knob of butter.

3.

Tilt the pan around so that the butter melts evenly over the base.

4.

Pour in the egg mixture and cook over medium heat.

5.

Lift the edges with a spatula so uncooked egg runs underneath.

6.

Cook until the omelette is set and golden.

7.

Loosen from pan with the spatula. Fold in half.

8.

Place on a serving plate. Garnish with parsley.

10 mins

makes
⅔ cup

CREAM CHEESE ICING

- 1 cup icing sugar
- 150 g spreadable cream cheese
- 1 tsp lemon juice

1.

Sift icing sugar into a bowl.

2.

Add cream cheese.

3.

Add lemon juice.

4.

Beat with electric beaters until combined.

- NOTE 1 -

Spread icing over cakes such as Carrot Cake, Marble Cake and Banana Cake, using a flat knife.

- NOTE 2 -

Cream cheese icing can be stored in fridge for up to 5 days.

BUTTERCREAM ICING

10–15 mins

makes ⅔ cup

- 2 cups icing sugar
- 115 g butter, softened
- ½ tsp vanilla essence
- 1–2 tbsp milk

1.

Sift icing sugar into a bowl.

2.

Using electric beaters, cream the butter with vanilla and half the icing sugar.

3.

Gradually beat in the remaining icing sugar until smooth. Add milk and beat well.

4.

Spread over your favourite cakes or cupcakes using a flat knife.

– VARIATION 1 –

To make Chocolate Buttercream Icing, sift 2 tbsp cocoa with the icing sugar.

– VARIATION 2 –

To make Lemon Buttercream Icing, beat 1 tsp finely grated lemon zest into the buttercream.

40 mins

makes
10

BUTTERMILK WAFFLES

- 2 large eggs, at room temperature
- 1 cup buttermilk
- ¾ cup milk
- 100 ml vegetable or canola oil
- 2 cups Edmonds self-raising flour
- 1½ tsp cinnamon
- ¼ cup caster sugar
- baking spray
- natural yoghurt, to serve
- diced fresh fruit, e.g. kiwifruit, banana, strawberries, to serve

1.

Blend eggs, buttermilk, milk and oil in a food processor.

2.

Transfer to a bowl and add flour, cinnamon and sugar. Mix well.

3.

Let mixture stand, covered, for 30 minutes before using (if possible).

4.

Preheat a waffle maker to desired temperature. Spray with baking spray.

5.

Place ¼ cup of the mix in the heated waffle maker. Cook until golden.

6.

Repeat with remaining batter. Serve with yoghurt and diced fruit.

PANCAKES

5–20 mins

serves 3–4

- 2 cups Edmonds standard flour
- 2 tbsp sugar
- ½ tsp salt
- 1 tsp Edmonds baking powder
- ½ tsp Edmonds baking soda
- 1½ cups whole milk
- 2 large eggs, at room temperature
- 3 tbsp butter, melted and cooled slightly
- extra butter, to grease

1.

Sieve flour, sugar, salt, baking powder and baking soda into a bowl.

2.

In a second bowl, whisk together milk, eggs and melted butter.

3.

Make a well in dry ingredients. Pour in wet ingredients. Stir gently until just combined. Set aside for 10 minutes.

4.

Heat a little butter in a non-stick frypan over medium heat.

5.

Pour ¼ cup portions of batter into the pan. Cook 2–3 minutes until surface bubbles start breaking.

6.

Using a thin, wide spatula, flip pancakes and cook 1–2 minutes until second side is golden brown.

7.

Repeat with remaining batter.

8.

Serve pancakes immediately with toppings of your choice, or keep warm in a preheated oven.

20 mins

serves
2–4

FRENCH TOAST

- 2 eggs, at room temperature
- 2 tbsp milk
- salt and pepper
- 4 slices toast-cut wholemeal or white bread

- butter, to grease
- maple syrup, to serve (optional)
- grilled bacon, to serve (optional)

1. 

Put eggs and milk in a bowl. Beat until combined.

2. 

Season with salt and pepper.

3. 

Cut each slice of bread in half diagonally, to make 2 triangles.

4. 

Melt a little butter in a frypan over low–medium heat.

5. 

Dip bread triangles in egg and milk mixture, one at a time.

6. 

Place in frypan. Cook for 2 minutes until underside is golden.

7. 

Turn and cook for a further 2 minutes.

8. 

Serve with maple syrup and grilled bacon, if you like.

GRANOLA

45 mins

makes
7 cups

- 3 cups wholegrain rolled oats
- 1 cup shredded coconut
- ½ cup wheatgerm
- ¼ cup hazelnuts or chopped brazil nuts
- ½ cup seeds, e.g. sunflower seeds, pumpkin seeds
- 1 tsp cinnamon
- ⅓ cup canola oil
- ⅓ cup runny honey
- 1 cup raisins or sultanas
- ¾ cup chopped dried apricots
- milk or yoghurt, fresh fruit such as berries or chopped banana, to serve

1.

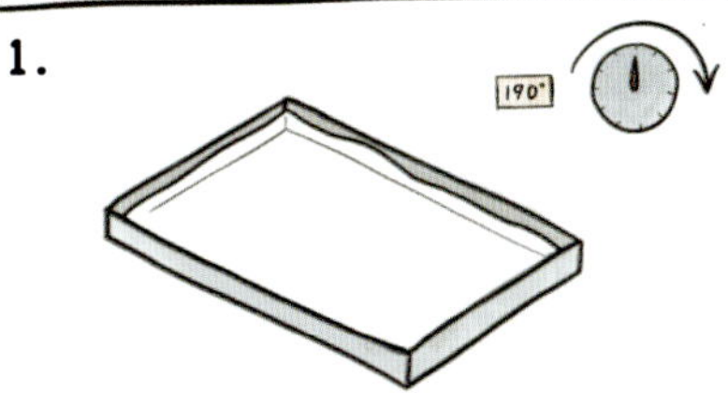

Preheat oven to 190°C.
Line a baking tray with baking paper.

2.

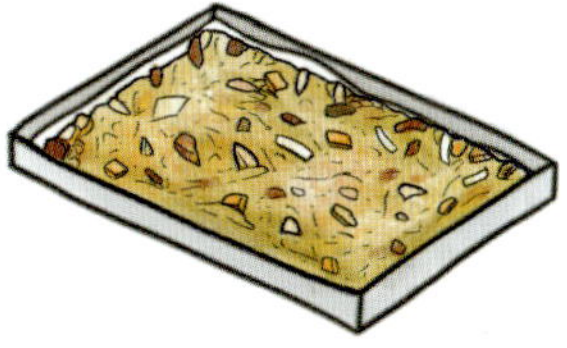

Combine oats, coconut, wheatgerm, nuts, seeds and cinnamon well in the baking tray.

3.

In a bowl, mix together the oil and honey.
Drizzle over the oats and mix gently.

4.

Bake 25–30 minutes or until golden.
Stir every 5 minutes (very important!).

5.

Cool and stir in the dried fruit. Serve with milk or yoghurt and fresh fruit.

- NOTE -

Store in an airtight container.

30 mins

makes
24

AFGHANS

- 200 g butter, softened
- ½ cup sugar
- 1¼ cups Edmonds standard flour
- ¼ cup cocoa
- 2 cups cornflakes

– CHOCOLATE ICING –

- 2 cups icing sugar
- 2 tbsp cocoa
- 25 g butter, softened
- 2 tbsp hot water
- ¼ tsp vanilla essence
- 24 walnuts (optional)

1.

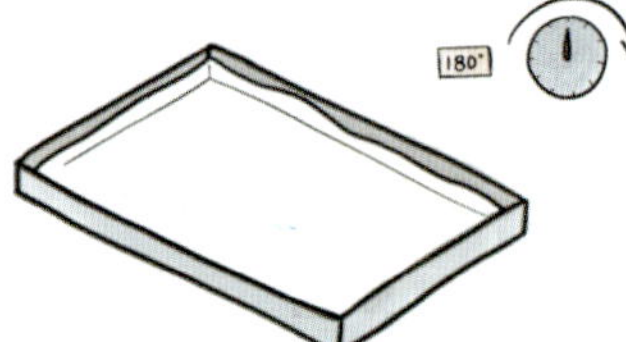

Preheat oven to 180°C. Line a
baking tray with baking paper.

2.

Cream the butter and sugar with
electric beaters until light and fluffy.

3.

Sift flour and cocoa into the creamed
mixture. Stir well. Fold in cornflakes.

4.

Spoon tablespoonfuls of the mixture
onto the tray, gently pressing together.

5.

Bake 15 minutes or until set.
Set aside to cool.

6.

For the icing, sift icing sugar and
cocoa. Add the butter.

7.

Add enough hot water to make the
icing spreadable. Mix in vanilla.

8.

When the biscuits are cold, ice and
decorate with a walnut, if you like.

ANZAC BISCUITS

- ½ cup Edmonds standard flour
- ⅓ cup sugar
- ⅔ cup finely desiccated coconut
- ¾ cup rolled oats

- 50 g butter
- 1 tbsp golden syrup
- ½ tsp Edmonds baking soda
- 2 tbsp boiling water

1.

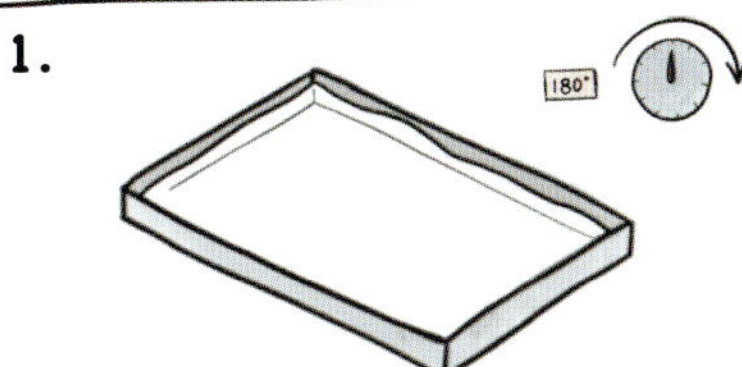

Preheat oven to 180°C.
Line a baking tray with baking paper.

2.

Combine flour, sugar, coconut and rolled oats.

3.

Melt butter and golden syrup.

4.

Dissolve baking soda in boiling water.
Add to the butter mixture and stir.

5.

Stir wet mixture into the dry ingredients.

6.

Place level tablespoonfuls of the mixture onto the prepared tray. Flatten with a fork.

7.

Bake for 15 minutes or until golden.

8.

Leave on tray for 5 minutes.
Transfer to a wire rack to cool.

35 mins

makes
25

CHOCOLATE CHIP COOKIES

- 125 g butter, softened
- ¼ cup sugar
- 3 tbsp sweetened condensed milk
- few drops of vanilla essence

- 1½ cups Edmonds standard flour
- 1 tsp Edmonds baking powder
- ½ cup chocolate chips

1.

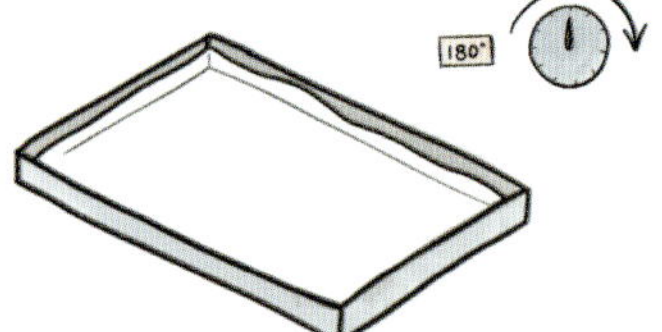

Preheat oven to 180°C. Line a baking tray with baking paper.

2.

Cream butter, sugar, condensed milk and vanilla with electric beaters until light and fluffy.

3.

Sift flour and baking powder. Mix into the creamed mixture.

4.

Stir in chocolate chips with a wooden spoon.

5.

Roll tablespoonfuls of mixture into balls.

6.

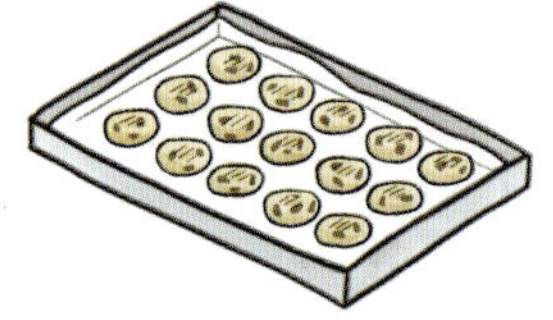

Place on the prepared tray. Flatten with a floured fork.

7.

Bake for 20 minutes until golden.

8.

Leave on tray for 1–2 minutes. Transfer to a wire rack to cool.

CHOCOLATE CRACKLES

40 mins

makes 24

- 250 g vegetable shortening
- 1 cup icing sugar
- ¼ cup cocoa
- 4 cups puffed rice breakfast cereal or cornflakes
- 1 cup desiccated coconut

1.

Melt vegetable shortening in a saucepan.

2.

Sift icing sugar and cocoa and add to the pan. Mix well.

3.

Tip in puffed rice or cornflakes and coconut.

4.

Stir everything together.

5.

Put spoonfuls into paper cupcake cases.

6.

Set in the fridge for 30 minutes.

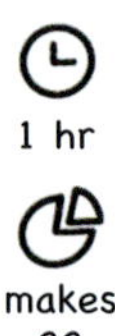

1 hr

makes 22

HOKEY POKEY COOKIES

- 125 g butter
- ½ cup sugar
- 1 tbsp golden syrup
- 1 tbsp milk
- 1½ cups Edmonds standard flour
- 1 tsp Edmonds baking soda

1.

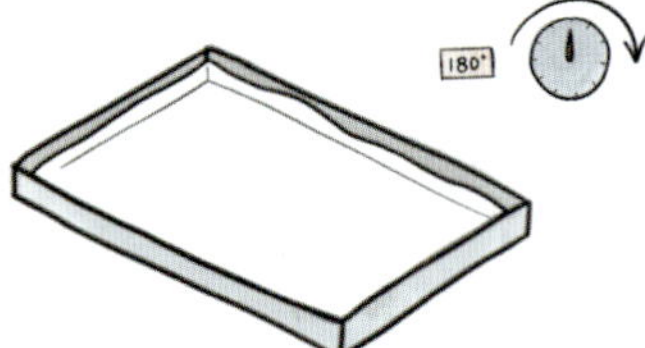

Preheat oven to 180°C. Line a baking tray with baking paper.

2.

Heat butter, sugar, golden syrup and milk over medium heat.

3.

Stir constantly until the butter melts and the mixture is almost boiling.

4.

Remove from heat. Allow to cool to lukewarm.

5.

Sift flour and baking soda. Add to the cooled mixture. Stir well.

6.

Roll tablespoonfuls of mixture into balls. Place on the prepared tray.

7.

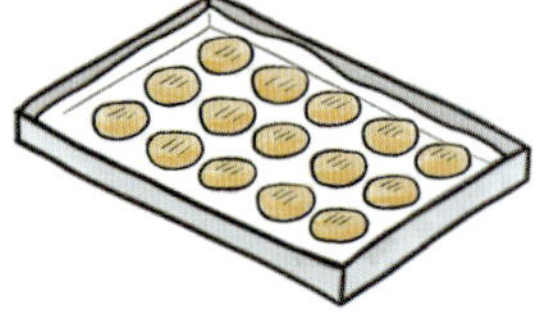

Flatten with a floured fork. Bake 15–20 minutes until golden brown.

8.

Leave on tray for 1–2 minutes. Transfer to a wire rack to cool.

MELTING MOMENTS

1 hr

makes 16

- 200 g butter, softened
- ¾ cup icing sugar
- 1 cup Edmonds standard flour
- 1 cup Edmonds Fielder's cornflour
- ½ tsp Edmonds baking powder
- Buttercream Icing (see page 53) or raspberry jam

1.

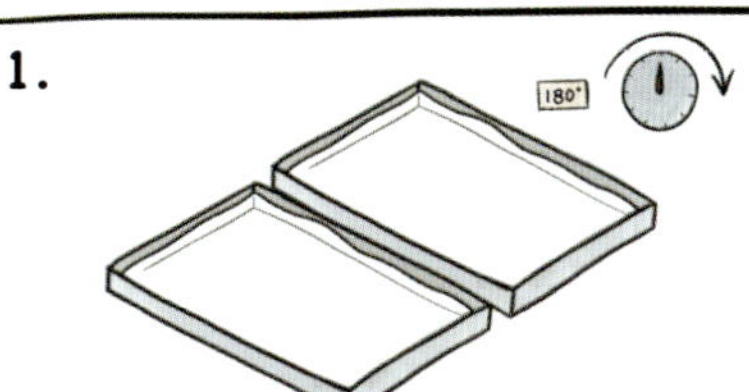

Preheat oven to 180°C. Line two baking trays with baking paper.

2.

Cream butter and icing sugar with electric beaters until light and fluffy.

3.

Sift flour, cornflour and baking powder. Add to mixture. Work together to form smooth dough.

4.

Roll heaped teaspoonfuls of dough into balls. Place on the prepared trays.

5.

Press down lightly with a floured fork.

6.

Bake for 20 minutes or until the bases are lightly golden.

7.

Leave on trays for 1–2 minutes. Transfer to a wire rack to cool.

8.

When cold, sandwich biscuits together with Buttercream Icing or raspberry jam.

1½–2 hrs

makes 30

SHORTBREAD

- 200 g butter, softened
- 1 cup icing sugar
- 1 cup Edmonds Fielder's cornflour
- 2 cups Edmonds standard flour

1.

Cream butter and icing sugar with electric beaters until light and fluffy.

2.

Sift cornflour and flour. Add to the butter mixture.

3.

Knead well on a floured surface, pushing with hands until the dough is smooth.

4.

Form dough into a log, wrap in greaseproof paper and chill for 30–40 minutes.

5.

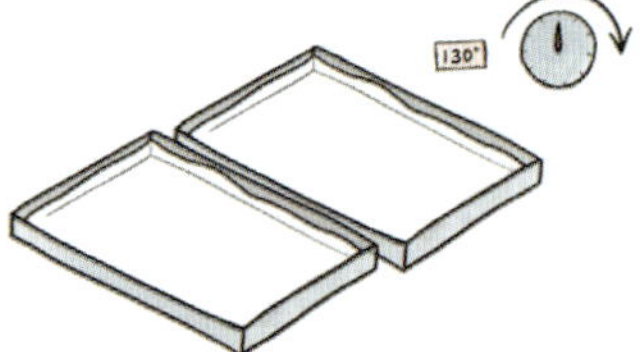

Preheat oven to 130°C. Line 2 trays with baking paper.

6.

Cut the dough log into 5 mm thick biscuits.

7.

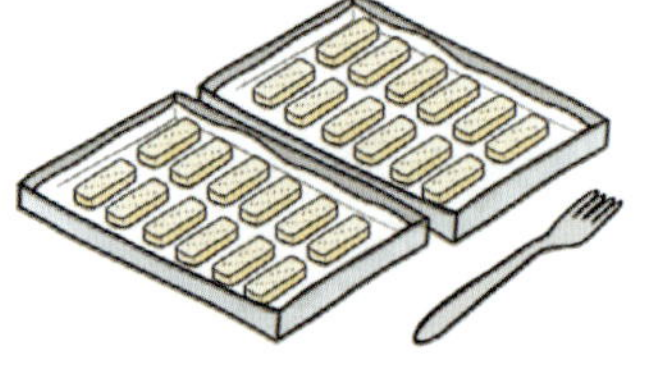

Place on lined trays and prick with a fork.

8.

Bake for 30 minutes until pale golden.

SNICKERDOODLE

30 mins

makes
20

- 125 g butter, softened
- ¾ cup sugar
- 1 egg, at room temperature
- 1 ⅓ cups Edmonds standard flour
- 1½ tsp Edmonds baking powder
- ⅛ tsp salt

– COATING –

- 2 tbsp sugar
- 2 tsp cinnamon

1.

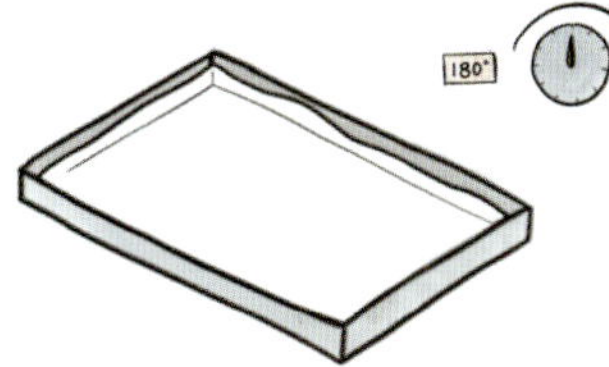

Preheat oven to 180°C.
Line a baking tray with baking paper.

2.

Cream butter and sugar with electric
beaters. Add egg. Beat well.

3.

Mix flour, baking powder and salt.
Add to egg mixture. Stir.

4.

Roll tablespoonfuls of mixture
into balls using lightly floured hands.

5.

For coating, combine sugar and cinnamon.

6.

Cover balls in cinnamon sugar.
Put 5 cm apart on the prepared tray.

7.

Bake for 8–10 minutes until
edges are golden.

8.

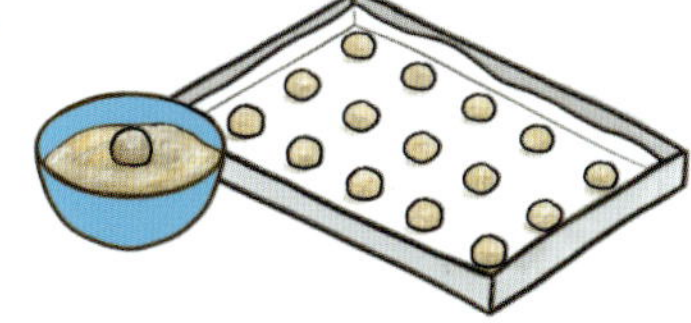

Leave on a tray for 1–2 minutes.
Transfer to a wire rack to cool.

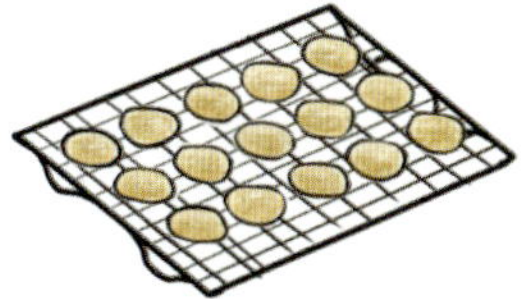

20 mins

makes
16

BUBBLE SLICE

- 160 g butter
- 1 cup sugar
- 4 tbsp honey
- 6 cups puffed rice breakfast cereal
- ½ cup chopped nuts or shredded coconut

1.

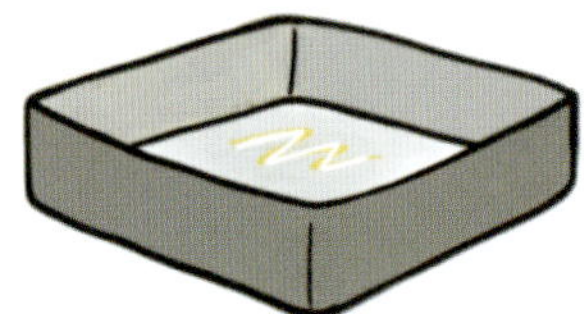

Grease a 20 cm square baking tin.

2.

Place butter, sugar and honey in large microwave-proof bowl.

3.

Microwave on high for 3 minutes, stir, then repeat twice more.

4.

The butter should be melted and the mixture just golden.

5.

Fold puffed rice and nuts or coconut into the mixture.

6.

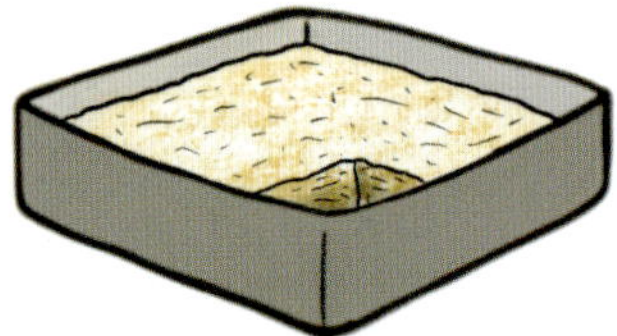

Press the mixture into the tin. Cut into slabs when just cool.

CHOCOLATE BROWNIE

1½ hrs

makes 20

- 150 g butter
- 1 cup cocoa
- 4 eggs, at room temperature
- 2 cups sugar
- 1 tsp vanilla essence
- ¾ cup Edmonds standard flour
- 1 tsp Edmonds baking powder
- 250 g dark chocolate, chopped
- icing sugar, to dust

1.

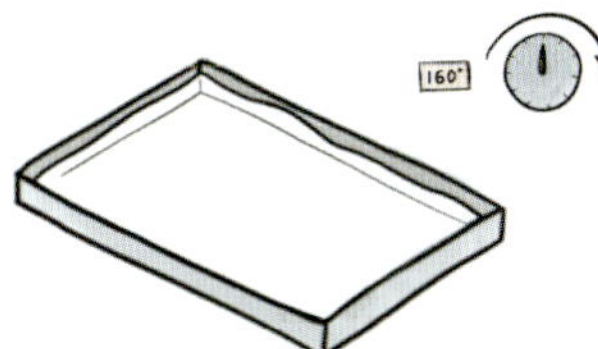

Preheat oven to 160°C. Grease and line a 27 cm x 18 cm shallow tin.

2.

Melt butter. Stir in cocoa. Add eggs one at a time, beating each time.

3.

Add sugar, vanilla, sifted flour, baking powder and chocolate. Stir well.

4.

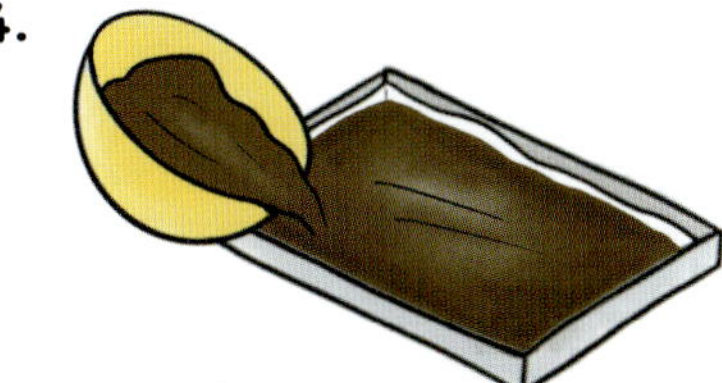

Pour the mixture into the prepared tin.

5.

Bake for 45–50 minutes until just firm when pressed in centre.

6.

Leave for 20 minutes in the tin then transfer to a wire rack to cool.

7.

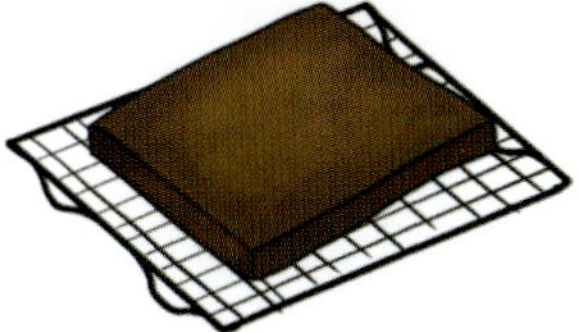

Remove baking paper and reverse onto another rack.

8.

When cold, dust with icing sugar and cut into squares.

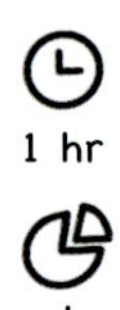

FLAPJACKS

- 250 g butter
- ½ cup caster sugar
- 3 tbsp honey
- 1 tbsp peanut butter
- 2½ cups rolled oats
- 1 cup shredded coconut
- ½ cup chopped apricots
- ¾ cup raisins
- 1 tsp cinnamon
- 70 g flaked almonds
- ¼ cup sunflower seeds

1.

Preheat oven to 160°C. Line a 20 cm x 30 cm tin with baking paper.

2.

Melt butter, sugar, honey and peanut butter. Stir. Do not boil.

3.

Mix remaining ingredients in a large bowl. Pour in butter mixture. Stir well.

4.

Tip into the prepared tin. Press down with a spatula to fill the whole tin.

5.

Bake until golden for no more than 40 minutes. (Check first at 35 minutes.)

6.

Allow to cool in the pan. Cut into slabs when completely cold.

CHOCOLATE CARAMEL SLICE

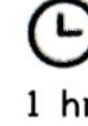

1 hr

makes 24

- BASE -

- 150 g butter
- 1 tbsp golden syrup
- ½ cup brown sugar
- 1 cup rolled oats
- 1 cup Edmonds standard flour
- 1 tsp Edmonds baking powder

- TOPPING -

- 1 cup brown sugar
- 2 tbsp sweetened condensed milk
- 2 tbsp butter
- 1 cup icing sugar
- 1 tbsp hot water
- Chocolate Icing (see page 58) or 100 g dark chocolate, melted

1.

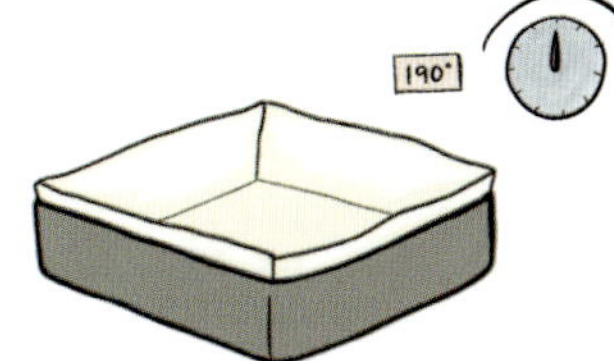

Preheat oven to 180°C. Grease and line a 20 cm cake tin.

2.

Melt butter, golden syrup and brown sugar.

3.

Add rolled oats, sifted flour and baking powder. Mix to form a firm dough.

4.

Press dough evenly into prepared tin with a spatula. Bake for 15 minutes.

5.

For the topping, heat brown sugar, condensed milk and butter until bubbling.

6.

Add icing sugar and water. Whisk to combine to make caramel.

7.

Remove base from oven. Spread with warm caramel filling. Cool in tin on wire rack.

8.

When cold, spread over Chocolate Icing or melted chocolate. Cut into slices when set.

45 mins

makes
24

GINGER CRUNCH

- BASE -

- ½ cup sugar
- 1½ cups Edmonds standard flour
- 1 tsp Edmonds baking powder
- 1 tsp ground ginger
- 125 g butter, cubed and softened

- GINGER ICING -

- 55 g butter
- 1 tbsp golden syrup
- 2 tsp ground ginger
- ½ cup icing sugar

1.

Preheat oven to 180°C. Grease and
line a 20 cm x 30 cm tin.

2.

Pulse dry ingredients in a food processor.
Add butter. Process until fine crumbs form.

3.

Tip into prepared tin. Spread evenly.
Press down firmly with fingers.

4.

Bake for 20–25 minutes until a pale,
golden brown.

5.

For the icing, gently heat butter, golden
syrup and ginger. Stir until melted.
Sift in icing sugar.

6.

Mix until the icing is well blended.

7.

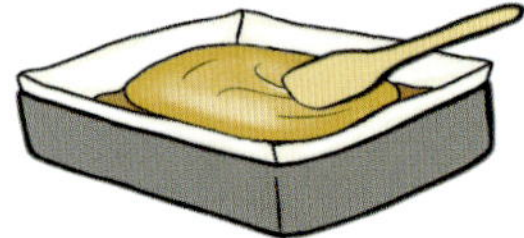

Remove tin from oven. Pour the icing
over the base. Spread in a thin layer.

8.

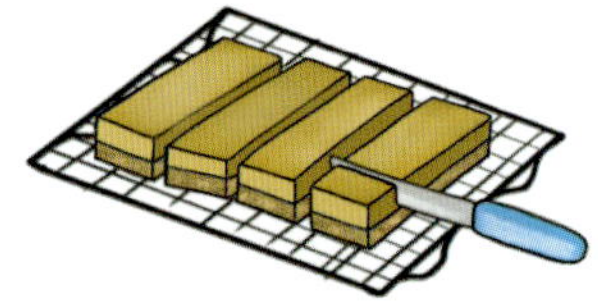

Turn out to cool on a wire rack.
Cut into fingers.

MUFFINS

30 mins

makes
12

- ¾ cup Edmonds wholemeal flour
- ¾ cup Edmonds standard flour
- 1 tsp Edmonds baking powder
- pinch of salt
- ½ cup brown sugar

- ½ cup chocolate chips
- 50 g butter, melted
- 1 egg, at room temperature
- ½ tsp Edmonds baking soda
- ¾ cup milk

1.

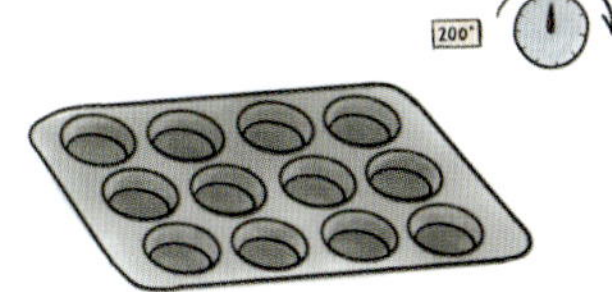

Preheat oven to 200°C.
Grease 12-hole muffin tin.

2.

Sift flours, baking powder and salt into a
bowl. Stir in sugar. Add chocolate chips.

3.

Mix cooled melted butter and egg in a
bowl. Dissolve baking soda in milk in a jug.

4.

Tip wet mixtures into dry mixture.
Mix quickly with a rounded knife.
Do not over-mix.

5.

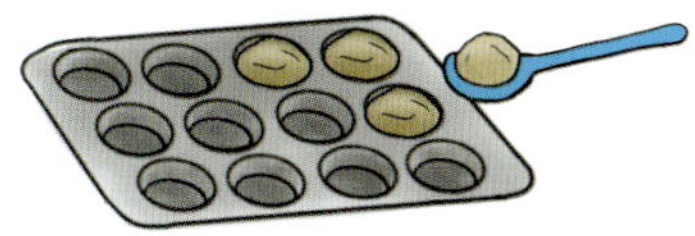

Spoon mixture into prepared muffin tins.

6.

Bake 12–15 minutes until risen and golden.
Cool on a wire rack.

- VARIATION 1 -

For banana muffins, add ½ cup mashed
banana after sifted ingredients.

- VARIATION 2 -

For berry muffins, add ½ cup frozen or
fresh berries after sifted ingredients.

CUPCAKES

- 125 g butter, softened
- 1 tsp vanilla essence
- ½ cup caster sugar
- 2 eggs, at room temperature
- 1 cup Edmonds standard flour
- 2 tsp Edmonds baking powder
- ¼ cup milk

1.

Preheat oven to 190°C. Put paper patty cases into a 12-hole muffin tin.

2.

Cream butter, vanilla and sugar with electric beaters until light and fluffy.

3.

Add eggs one at a time, beating well each time.

4.

Sift flour and baking powder. Fold gently into creamed mixture. Stir in milk.

5.

Spoon the mixture into paper cases. Bake 15 minutes until cakes spring back when lightly touched.

6.

Transfer to a wire rack to cool. Ice and decorate as you wish.

- VARIATION 1 -

For Pink Icing Cupcakes, use the Buttercream Icing recipe (see page 53) and add ¼ teaspoon red food colouring at the same time as the vanilla essence.

- VARIATION 2 -

For Chocolate Cupcakes, replace 2 tablespoons of measured flour with 2 tablespoons cocoa. Ice with Chocolate Icing (see page 58) or Chocolate Buttercream Icing (see page 53).

SCONES

20 mins

makes
12

- 3 cups Edmonds standard flour
- 5 tsp Edmonds baking powder
- ¼ tsp salt

- 75 g cold butter
- about 1¼ cups milk
- extra milk, about ¼ cup

1.

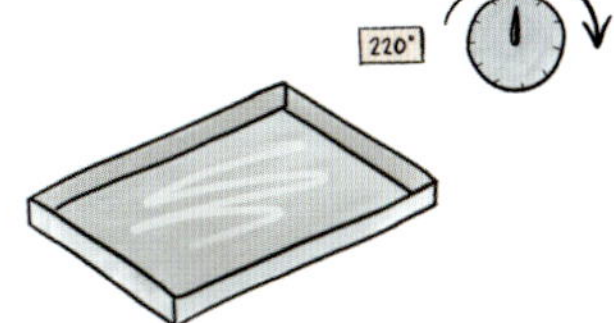

Preheat oven to 220°C.
Grease or flour a baking tray.

2.

Sift flour, baking powder and
salt into a bowl.

3.

Rub in butter with fingertips until the
mixture resembles fine breadcrumbs.

4.

Add milk. Quickly mix with a rounded
knife to form a soft, sticky dough.

5.

Scrape dough onto prepared
baking tray. Flour the top.

6.

Quickly pat the dough to 2 cm thickness.

7.

Cut into 12 even pieces. Place 2 cm apart.
Brush tops with the extra milk.

8.

Bake 10 minutes until golden. Cover with
a clean tea towel. Cool on a wire rack.

20 mins

makes 18

- 1 cup Edmonds standard flour
- 1 tsp Edmonds baking powder
- ¼ tsp salt
- 1 egg, at room temperature
- ¼ cup sugar
- about ¾ cups milk
- 3 tbsp butter, melted and cooled slightly

1.

Sift flour, baking powder and salt into a bowl.

2.

Whisk egg and sugar until pale and thick.

3.

Add egg mixture and milk to dry ingredients.

4.

Mix until just combined. Add more milk if needed.

5.

Gently heat a little butter in a non-stick frypan.

6.

Drop in tablespoonfuls of mixture.

7.

When bubbles appear, turn over and cook the other side until golden.

8.

Place in a clean tea towel to keep warm. Serve warm with jam and a little whipped cream.

BANANA LOAF

1½ hrs

makes
1

- 1¾ cups Edmonds self-raising flour
- ¼ tsp Edmonds baking soda
- ¼ tsp salt
- ½ cup sugar

- 2 eggs, at room temperature
- ¼ cup milk
- 75 g butter, melted
- 1 cup mashed banana

1.

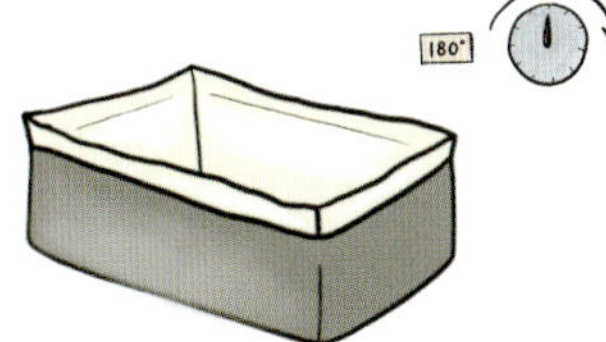

Preheat oven to 180°C. Grease and line a 26 cm × 13 cm loaf tin.

2.

Sift flour, baking soda and salt into a bowl. Mix in sugar.

3.

In another bowl, beat eggs. Stir in milk, butter and banana.

4.

Pour wet ingredients into the dry ingredients.

5.

Stir until just combined.

6.

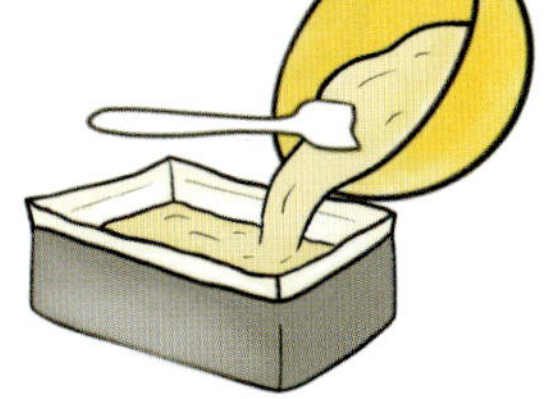

Spoon mixture into the prepared loaf tin.

7.

Bake 45–55 minutes or until a skewer inserted in centre comes out clean.

8.

Leave in tin for 10 minutes. Transfer to a wire rack to cool.

55 mins

serves 10

CARROT CAKE

- ¾ cup canola oil
- 1 cup firmly packed brown sugar
- 3 eggs, at room temperature
- 3 cups firmly packed grated carrot (about 3 large carrots)
- ½ cup chopped walnuts
- 2 cups Edmonds standard flour
- 2 tsp Edmonds baking powder
- ½ tsp Edmonds baking soda
- 1 tsp cinnamon
- Cream Cheese Icing (see page 52)
- chopped walnuts, pumpkin seeds, dried pineapple, pawpaw to garnish (optional)

1.

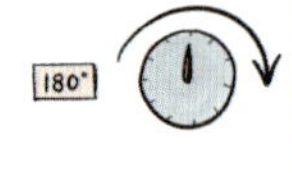

Preheat oven to 180°C. Grease and line a 20 cm round cake tin.

2.

Beat oil, sugar and eggs for 5 minutes with electric beaters until thick. Fold in carrot and walnuts.

3.

Sift flour, baking powder, baking soda and cinnamon. Fold into wet mixture.

4.

Put mixture in tin. Bake for 1 hour or until skewer inserted in centre comes out clean.

5.

Stand in tin for 10 minutes. Transfer to a wire rack to cool.

6.

Ice and sprinkle with walnuts, seeds and dried fruit pieces.

CHOCOLATE CAKE

 1½ hrs

 serves 8

- 175 g butter, softened
- 1¾ cups sugar
- 1 tsp vanilla essence
- 3 eggs, at room temperature
- ½ cup cocoa
- 2 cups Edmonds standard flour
- 2 tsp Edmonds baking powder
- 1 cup milk
- Chocolate Buttercream Icing (see page 53)
- icing sugar (optional)

1.

Preheat oven to 180°C. Grease and line a 22 cm deep round cake tin.

2.

Cream butter, sugar and vanilla with electric beaters until light and fluffy.

3.

Add eggs one at a time, beating well each time.

4.

Sift cocoa, flour and baking powder into a bowl.

5.

Add to creamed mixture alternately with the milk. Pour into prepared tin.

6.

Bake for 45–55 minutes or until cake springs back when lightly touched.

7.

Leave in tin for 10 minutes. Transfer to a wire rack to cool.

8.

Ice with Chocolate Buttercream Icing or dust with icing sugar.

1 hr

serves 8

MARBLE CAKE

- 3 eggs, at room temperature
- ¾ cup caster sugar
- 1 cup Edmonds standard flour
- 1 tsp Edmonds baking powder
- 50 g butter

- 2 tbsp boiling water
- 1 tbsp cocoa
- 2–3 drops red food colouring
- Buttercream Icing (see page 53)
- icing sugar (optional)

1.

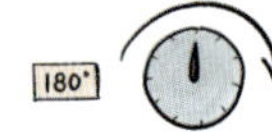

Preheat oven to 180°C.
Grease and line a 20 cm round cake tin.

2.

Beat eggs until frothy.
Beat in sugar gradually until
mixture is very thick and pale.

3.

Sift flour and baking powder and
fold into egg mixture. Mix in butter
melted with boiling water.

4.

Divide batter into thirds. Stir cocoa
into one third, add colouring to another.
Leave the last third plain.

5.

Spoon the mixtures in stripes into tin.
Swirl together with a knife.

6.

Bake for 20–25 minutes or until cake
springs back when lightly touched.

7.

Leave in tin for 10 minutes.
Transfer to a wire rack to cool.

8.

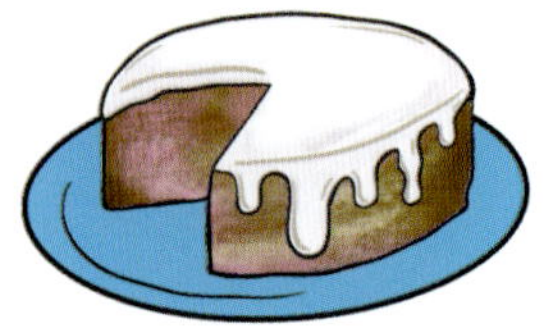

Ice with Buttercream Icing or
dust with icing sugar.

BANANA CAKE

2 hrs

serves
8

- 2½ cups Edmonds self-raising flour
- 1 tsp Edmonds baking soda
- 1 cup caster sugar
- 4 lightly beaten eggs, at room temperature
- 2½ cups mashed bananas (about 4 bananas)
- 1 cup vegetable oil
- Cream Cheese Icing (see page 52)

1.

Preheat oven to 160°C. Grease and line a 20 cm round cake tin.

2.

Sift flour and baking soda into a bowl.

3.

Make a well in the centre and stir in sugar, eggs, banana and oil.

4.

Mix gently to form a smooth batter. Pour into lined tin.

5.

Bake for 1½ hours or until a skewer inserted in centre comes out clean.

6.

Cool completely, then spread over Cream Cheese Icing using a flat knife.

50 mins

serves 6

SPONGE CAKE

- 3 eggs, at room temperature
- pinch of salt
- ¾ cup caster sugar
- 1 cup Edmonds standard flour
- 1 tsp Edmonds baking powder
- 50 g butter, melted
- 4 tbsp jam and 200 ml whipped cream, to serve

1.

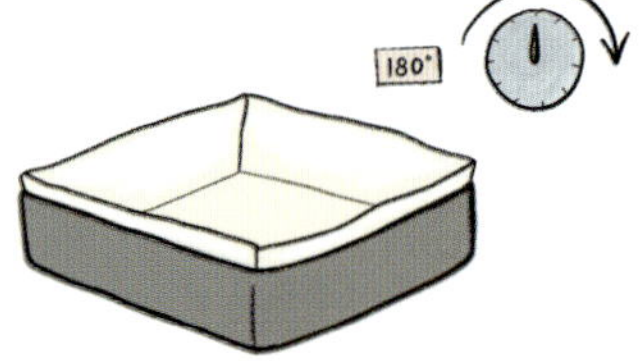

Preheat oven to 180°C. Grease and line a 20 cm square cake tin.

2.

Use electric beaters to beat eggs with salt until very foamy, about 1 minute.

3.

Add sugar gradually, beating well.

4.

Keep beating for 5 minutes until the mixture is very pale and fluffy.

5.

Sift flour and baking powder. Sift again onto egg mixture. Fold through gently.

6.

Fold in melted butter. Combine well. Pour mixture into lined tin.

7.

Bake for 25–30 minutes until golden and cake springs back when lightly touched.

8.

Cool on a wire rack. When cool, carefully slice the cake in half. Spread one half with jam, then cream, and place the other half on top.

BAKED DOUGHNUTS

30 mins

makes
12–16

- 2 cups Edmonds standard flour
- 3 tsp Edmonds baking powder
- ¼ cup sugar
- 125 g very cold butter, grated
- ¾ cup milk
- 1 large egg, at room temperature

– COATING –

- ¾ cup sugar
- 4 tsp cinnamon
- 80 g butter, melted

1.

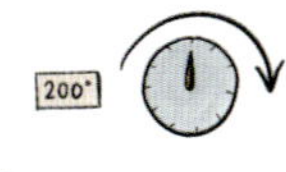

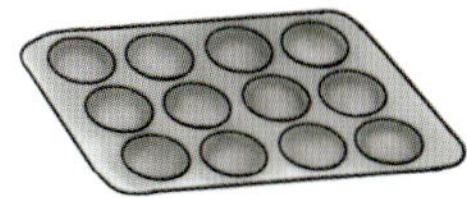

Preheat oven to 200°C. Grease a 12-hole round-based muffin tin.

2.

Sift flour and baking powder. Stir in sugar. Quickly stir in butter with a knife.

3.

Whisk together milk and egg. Pour into dry ingredients.

4.

Blend with a knife or spatula (not hands).

5.

With lightly floured hands, place balls of mixture in muffin holes.

6.

Bake for 10 minutes until golden and crispy.

7.

Combine sugar and cinnamon.

8.

Roll warm doughnuts in melted butter, then in sugar and cinnamon.

MERINGUE NESTS

1½ hrs

serves
6

- 4 egg whites, at room temperature
- 1½ cups caster sugar
- 1 tbsp Edmonds Fielder's cornflour
- 1 tsp white vinegar
- 1 tsp vanilla essence
- whipped cream, to serve
- seasonal fresh fruit and/or grated chocolate, to serve

1.

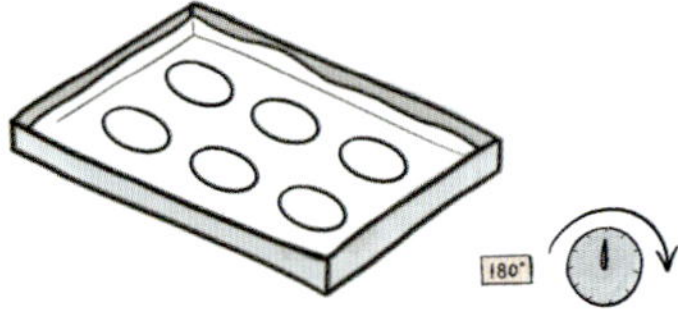

Preheat oven to 180°C. Draw six 10 cm circles on a large baking paper sheet. Place on a tray.

2.

Beat egg whites with electric beaters until soft peaks form.

3.

Gradually add sugar, beating constantly until thick and glossy.

4.

Combine cornflour, vinegar and vanilla. Add to egg mixture. Beat on high for 5 minutes.

5.

Divide mixture evenly onto the circles, spreading to just within edges.

6.

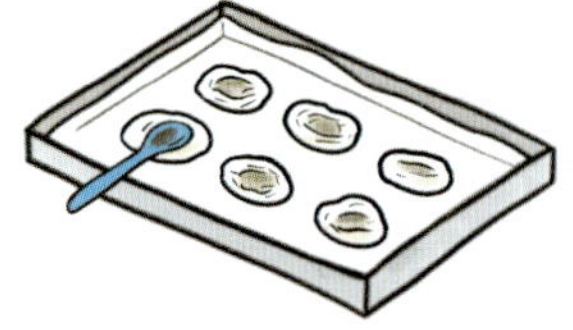

Using the back of a tablespoon, make a slight hollow in each of the centres.

7.

Put in oven. Turn down to 100°C. Bake for 50 minutes. Turn off oven and open the door slightly.

8.

When cold, decorate with cream, fruit and grated chocolate.

Apple Crumble

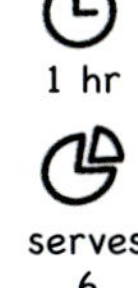

1 hr

serves 6

- 6 apples, medium sized
- ½ cup water
- 1 tsp lemon juice
- 1 tsp grated lemon rind
- 1 tsp cinnamon
- ¾ cup Edmonds standard flour
- 1 cup brown sugar
- 125 g butter
- whipped cream, to serve

1.

Preheat oven to 180°C.
Peel, core and slice the apples.

2.

Spread apple in a large pie dish.

3.

Sprinkle over water, lemon juice,
lemon rind and cinnamon.

4.

Put flour and brown sugar in
mixing bowl.

5.

Chop up butter and add.

6.

With clean fingers, rub it in until
it all looks crumbly.

7.

Sprinkle crumbs all over the top.
Bake for 40-45 minutes.

8.

Serve hot with whipped cream.

15 mins

serves
4

CARAMEL ICE-CREAM SUNDAE

- 125 g butter
- ¾ cup brown sugar
- 1½ tbsp Edmonds Fielder's cornflour
- 1 cup water
- 1 tbsp golden syrup
- ½ cup cream
- 8 scoops ice-cream

– TOPPINGS –

- chopped nuts
- grated chocolate
- marshmallows
- chopped banana
- glacé cherries
- wafer biscuits

1.

Heat butter and sugar in a saucepan. Stir until sugar dissolves.

2.

Boil for 3 minutes, stirring occasionally. Remove from heat.

3.

In a bowl, mix cornflour, water and golden syrup until smooth.

4.

Add to butter mixture. Bring back to the boil.

5.

Stir constantly for 2 minutes.

6.

Remove from heat and mix in the cream.

7.

Serve 2 scoops of ice-cream topped with caramel sauce.

8.

Top the sundae with your choice of toppings.

FRUIT SORBET

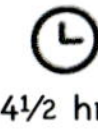
4½ hrs

serves
4

- 500 g summer fruit, such as grapes, plums, strawberries
- ½ cup sugar
- 1 cup water
- ¼ cup lemon juice
- 2 egg whites, at room temperature

1.

Purée fruit of your choice in a blender. Strain to remove skin and seeds.

2.

Combine sugar and water. Heat gently. Stir until the sugar dissolves.

3.

Allow to cool. Combine with fruit purée and lemon juice.

4.

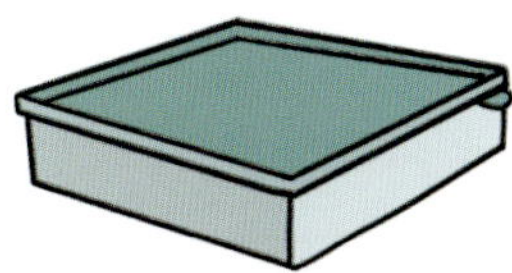

Pour into a shallow freezer-safe container. Cover.

5.

Freeze until the mixture starts to freeze on top and sides.

6.

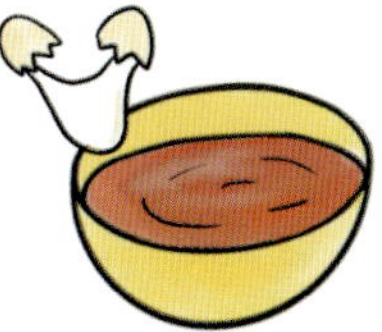

Transter to a bowl and add egg whites.

7.

Beat until well combined and fluffy.

8.

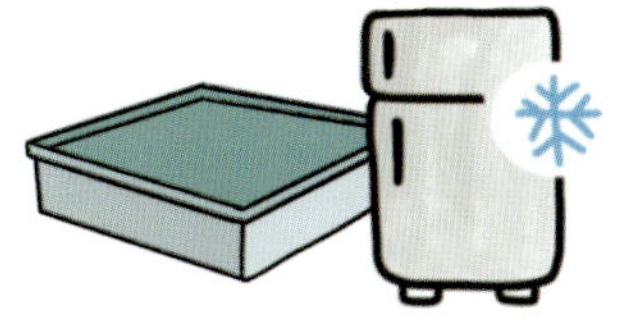

Return to container. Freeze until set, about 4 hours.

2 hrs

serves
6

FRUIT SALAD

- 3 or 4 types of ripe fruit, cut into bite-sized pieces

- SYRUP -

- 2 slices fresh ginger
- sprigs of fresh mint
- 3 tbsp sugar
- 6 tbsp water

1.

Mix fruit pieces together in a bowl.

2.

Put ginger and mint in a cup.

3.

Bring sugar and water to a simmer.

4.

Stir until sugar dissolves.

5.

Pour syrup into cup and leave to cool.

6.

Strain mint and ginger and pour a little syrup over the fruit salad.

BLISS BALLS

1 hr

makes 16

- 1 cup roughly chopped soft pitted dates
- ½ cup shredded coconut
- 1 tbsp chopped crystallised ginger
- 1 tbsp honey
- 1 tbsp cocoa
- ½ tsp ground ginger
- 4 tbsp currants or raisins

- COATING -

- cocoa
- grated chocolate
- toasted coconut
- finely chopped nuts

1.

Pulse ingredients in a food processor until well mixed but slightly lumpy.

2.

Add a little water if the mixture seems too crumbly.

3.

Taste for flavour and adjust if you like.

4.

Roll into 16 balls.

5.

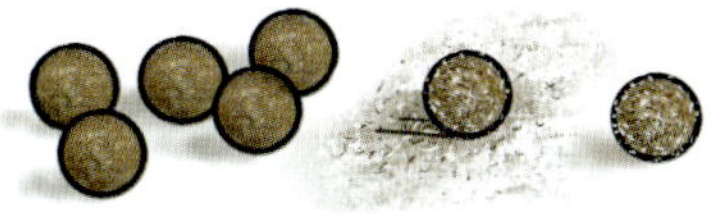

Roll balls in cocoa, grated chocolate, toasted coconut or finely chopped nuts.

6.

Chill until firm and store in the fridge.

1 hr

makes 36

COCONUT ICE

- ½ cup milk
- 25 g butter
- 3 cups icing sugar
- ¼ tsp salt
- ¾ cup desiccated coconut
- few drops red food colouring

1.

Grease a 20 cm square tin.

2.

Gently heat milk, butter, icing sugar and salt.

3.

Stir constantly for 10 minutes until the sugar dissolves.

4.

Bring to the boil. Simmer until the mixture is soft (114°C on a sugar thermometer).

5.

Remove from the heat. Mix in coconut. Cool for 10 minutes.

6.

Put half the mixture in a bowl. Add food colouring.

7.

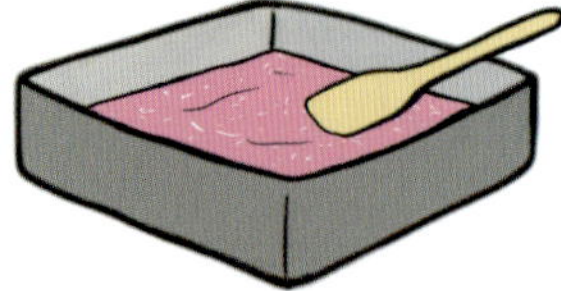

Beat with a wooden spoon until mixture thickens. Spread on base of the tin.

8.

Beat white portion until thick. Spread over pink mixture. Cool. Cut into squares.

RUSSIAN FUDGE

2 hrs

makes 36

- ½ cup milk
- 3 cups sugar
- ½ cup sweetened condensed milk
- 125 g butter
- ⅛ tsp salt
- 1 tbsp golden syrup
- 2 tsp vanilla essence

1.

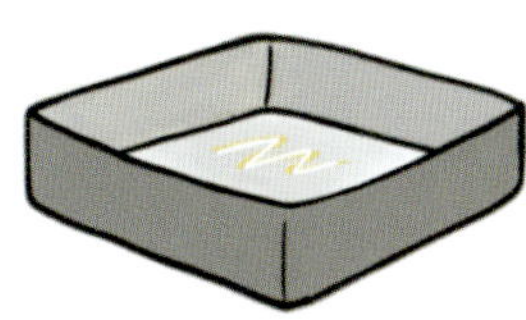

Lightly grease a 30 cm square tin.

2.

Gently heat milk and sugar. Stir constantly for 10 minutes until sugar dissolves.

3.

Add condensed milk, butter, salt and golden syrup. Stir until butter melts.

4.

Boil for 5 minutes until soft (114°C on a sugar thermometer). Stir occasionally.

5.

Remove from heat. Add vanilla. Allow to cool 2–3 minutes.

6.

Beat with a wooden spoon or electric beaters for 3 minutes until thick.

7.

Check every 30 seconds that mixture still levels out when removing spoon.

8.

Pour into the prepared tin and mark into squares. Cut when cold.

1 hr

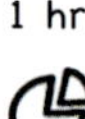
serves
6

CARAMEL POPCORN

- 2 tbsp oil
- ⅓ cup popping corn
- 200 g butter
- ⅔ cup firmly packed brown sugar
- 1½ tsp vanilla essence
- ¼ tsp baking soda

1.

Heat oil in saucepan over high heat.
Cover a baking tray with foil.

2.

Add corn to the pan and cover.
Shake until popping stops.

3.

Tip popcorn into a large bowl.
Shake and remove any un-popped corn.

4.

Melt butter. Add sugar and stir.

5.

Keep stirring until mixture boils,
then boil for 4 minutes.

6.

Mix in vanilla, then boil for 1 minute.
Add baking soda. Stir.

7.

Stir mixture through bowl of
popcorn to coat.

8.

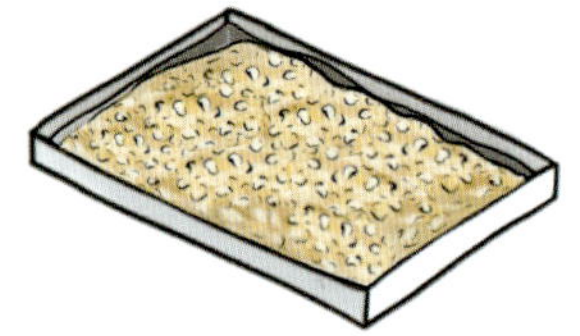

Pour popcorn onto tray. Let it cool.

FRUIT SMOOTHIE

- 3 tbsp natural yoghurt
- ½ cup mixed berries
- 1 scoop vanilla ice-cream
  or frozen yoghurt
- 2 cups cold milk
- 1 banana
- 1 tbsp honey (optional)

1.

Place all ingredients in a blender.

2.

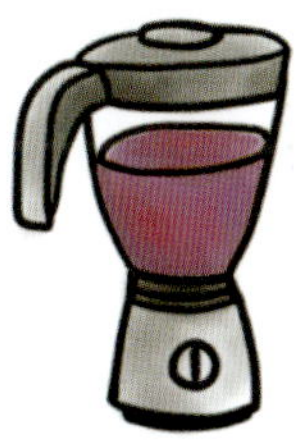

Blend until smooth.

3.

Pour into 2 tall glasses and serve.

- TIP -

Use a frozen banana for thicker texture.

- VARIATION 1 -

To make a green smoothie,
swap the berries for 1 cup of
baby spinach leaves.

- VARIATION 2 -

To make a peanut butter and chocolate
smoothie, swap the berries for 3 teaspoons
peanut butter, and add ½ tablespoon cocoa.

WEIGHTS & MEASURES

- New Zealand standard metric cup and spoon measures are used in all recipes.
- All measurements are level.
- Use measuring cups or jugs for liquid measures and sets of 1 cup, ½ cup, ⅓ cup and ¼ cup measures for dry ingredients.
- Brown sugar measurements are firmly packed, so that the sugar will hold the shape of the cup when tipped out.
- Size 6 eggs (53g) are used as the standard size unless otherwise stated.

ABBREVIATIONS	STANDARD MEASURES
tsp = teaspoon	1 cup = 250 ml
tbsp = tablespoon	1 L = 4 cups
L = litre	1 tbsp = 15 ml (note an Australian tbsp is 20 ml)
ml = millilitre	
cm = centimetre	1 tsp = 5 ml
mm = millimetre	½ tsp = 2.5 ml
g = gram	¼ tsp = 1.25 ml
°C = degrees Celsius	

OVEN HINTS

- Position your oven racks before turning the oven on.
- Oven positions (check your oven manual first, as it may have specific guidelines):
    - Bottom of oven: use for slow cooking and low-temperature cooking
    - Middle of oven: for moderate-temperature cooking
    - Above middle: for quick cooking and high-temperature cooking
- Fan-forced ovens: refer to the manufacturer's directions, as the models vary. As a general guide, subtract 20°C from recommended conventional oven temperature.
- Preheat the oven to required temperature before food preparation.
- Cooking temperatures and times are a guide only, as oven temperatures may vary.

USING THE RECIPES

- Read through each recipe carefully before starting. Check that you have all the ingredients you require.
- Preheat the oven before you start cooking. Remember to check the oven rack positions.
- Prepare tins, dishes or trays before cooking.
- Cooking temperatures and times, and number of serves or quantities made are given at the start of each recipe. Note, though, that oven temperatures may vary in individual ovens so they are a guide only.